LEADERSHIP FOR COMMUNITY EMPOWERMENT: A SOURCE BOOK

LEADERSHIP FOR COMMUNITY EMPOWERMENT: A SOURCE BOOK

by

Donna M. Schmitt
Assistant Professor of Educational Leadership and
Director, Center for Community Education
Eastern Michigan University

and

Donald C. Weaver
Professor of Educational Leadership and
Director, Center for Community Leadership Training
Western Michigan University

PENDELL
PUBLISHING
COMPANY

iii

LIBRARY OF CONGRESS
CATALOGING IN PUBLICATION DATA

Edited By
Donna M. Schmitt
and
Donald C. Weaver

LEADERSHIP FOR
COMMUNITY EMPOWERMENT:
A SOURCE BOOK

Includes Index
1. Community Leadership   I. Title
              301.155   78-70715
ISBN 0-87812-163-3

iv

To our students — past, present and future — whose leadership makes the achievement of "community" a viable goal in our time.

TABLE OF CONTENTS

LIST OF CONTRIBUTING AUTHORS:

DR. RICHARD AULT
  Management and Organization Development
  General Motors Corporation
  Detroit, Michigan

DR. JAMES DIXON, II
  Director
  Community Education Training Project
  Southern Illinois University at Edwardsville
  Edwardsville, Illinois

DR. THOMAS L. FISH
  Director
  Community Education Center
  College of St. Thomas
  St. Paul, Minnesota

DR. BARRY FITZGERALD
  Dean
  College of Advanced Education
  Ballarat, Australia

DR. GLORIA A. GREGG
  Director
  Center for Community Education
  Montana State University
  Bozeman, Montana

DR. JOHN B. JEFFREY
  Principal
  Potterville Middle School
  Potterville Public Schools
  Potterville, Michigan

DR. LLOYD E. McCLEARY
  Professor of Educational Administration
  University of Utah
  Salt Lake City, Utah

DR. BRIAN MILLER
  Coordinator
  Southwest Regional Center for Community Education Development
  Arizona State University
  Tempe, Arizona

DR. SIDNEY L. MILLER
  Consultant
  Institute for Community Education Development
  Ball State University
  Muncie, Indiana

DR. EVERETTE NANCE
  Director
  Midwest Community Education Development Center
  University of Missouri
  St. Louis, Missouri

DR. MICHAEL T. ORAVECZ
  Assistant Professor
  Technical and Community College
  The University of Akron
  Akron, Ohio

DR. STEVE R. PARSON
  Director
  Cooperative Extension Program for Community Education
  Virginia Polytechnic Institute and State University
  Blacksburg, Virginia

DR. CHARLES F. PORTER
  Director
  Community Education Center
  Colorado State University
  Fort Collins, Colorado

DR. DONNA M. SCHMITT
  Director
  Center for Community Education
  Eastern Michigan University
  Ypsilanti, Michigan

DR. ERIC C. SMITH
  Coordinator
  Community Education
  Wisconsin Department of Public Instruction
  Madison, Wisconsin

DR. LEE. K. VAUGHT
  Associate Director
  Center for Community Leadership Training
  Western Michigan University
  Kalamazoo, Michigan

DR. DONALD C. WEAVER
Director
Center for Community Leadership Training
Western Michigan University
Kalamazoo, Michigan

DR. LAWRENCE R. WILDER
Director of Federal Projects
Clovis Unified School District
Clovis, California

DR. GEORGE C. WOOD, JR.
Consultant
Institute for Community Education Development
Ball State University
Muncie, Indiana

FIGURES

FOREWORD

Community education has, at long last, found a place of significance among the priorities of school administrators, board members, and scholars on college campuses. As evidenced from recent legislative enactments in the nation's capital and in the statehouses across the nation, even the politicians are seeing a higher priority for community education. The fastest growing segment of higher education is in the community college sector. And this comes from the facility of these institutions to meet the needs of the communities which they serve. In the years to come, community education will continue to grow and it will become an even higher concern of school and college administrators.

This book of readings makes available to the student and the practitioner the best thinking of the authorities in the field of community education. The "what it is and how to do it" questions are largely answered in this unusually comprehensive treatise on this most timely topic. The authors have made a significant contribution to the literature on community education, and the reader is the benefactor of this intensive drawing together of what community education is all about and how it can be enhanced in the nation's schools and colleges.

T. H. Bell
Commissioner of Higher Education for
    the State of Utah
                    and
Former U. S. Commissioner of Education

INTRODUCTION

Recent years have seen a tremendous growth and development of strategies for building community input into decision-making, and for assisting the community to mobilize its collective strength in an enabling effort that provides community self-direction. Almost all Federal and much individual state legislation of the last several years has emphasized this aspect by requiring various vehicles of community analysis and involvement, such as community councils, open forums, town hall meetings, and advisory committees that are representative of the community. Community groups themselves are actively seeking more avenues for influence, as witnessed in the latest rise of cause-related organizations. Social institutions have thus sought to utilize constituency elements in the shaping of the agencies that serve the community, and in the programs that these agencies deliver. This has developed into an overall effort at community empowerment, an attempt to assist the community to assess its own needs and resources, and to relate these needs and resources to each other in a meaningful and effective manner.

One of the most comprehensive philosophies that has been built on the empowerment model has been the theory and practice of community education. The recent surge of growth in the practice of community cducation has lead to new interest in the exploration of both the philosophical and practical ramifications of the concept.

The core of the successful practice of community education lies within the quality of leadership that implements that practice. Thus, this book of readings attempts to analyze, in depth, various aspects of community education leadership, to determine those leadership skills and functions that are essential to success in community empowerment.

This source book is presented in five parts, each dealing with one aspect of community education leadership. Part I: "The Concept of Community Education" explores the philosophical underpinnings of the practice. Commitment to the concept as related to the development of its practice is discussed. The role of various initiation strategies and loci are also included in this section. Part II: "The Community Educator" reviews the practitioner from various points of view, including competency assessments, leadership styles, leadership roles, and leadership behaviors. "The Arena in Which Community Education is Practiced" is the topic of Part III. The community itself is analyzed as a social system that requires political skills on the part of the community educator. "Strategies for Community Education Leadership" are examined in Part IV, including community involvement, indigenous leadership training, resource management, processing

PART I

THE CONCEPT OF
COMMUNITY EDUCATION

skills, organization development, social interaction, and grantsmanship. Finally, Part V: "The National Network for Promotion of Community Education" reviews statewide and Federal efforts, as well as those of the C. S. Mott Foundation, in the development of community education.

It should be noted that the individual readings or chapters, while organized into thematic sections, are each to be considered as separate and independent entities. The thoughts and ideas expressed are those of the individual authors. However, we do believe that the critical analysis and comparison of the individual readings with each other as well as with the reader's own thoughts should have a synergistic effect, and lead the reader to new theories and conclusions.

It is hoped that these readings will be utilized in the training and preparation of leaders in the practice of community education. It is our belief that the training of leaders in community education is the most important function required to insure continuation of viable community education programs and processes leading to community empowerment in the years ahead. Thus, this book is intended to provide raw material for the improvement of that training.

DMS
DCW

"However fervently expressed, commitment alone does not insure the resolution of the critical social problems facing either the developed or the developing nations of the world. Leadership is required — leadership not only committed to making the world a better place for mankind but leadership capable of conceptualizing the interrelationships among the elements which comprise community and leadership trained in the skills required to operationalize the tenets of the community education faith." — *Weaver*

Chapter 1

Leadership as the Community Mobilizer

by
Donald C. Weaver

LEADERSHIP AS THE COMMUNITY MOBILIZER

COMMITMENT CHARACTERIZES THE MOVEMENT

Many of those who subscribe to the concept of community education express faith that it can contribute to the resolution of the critical societal problems facing America and other developed nations of the world.

Totten and Manley (1969) said:

We have so much faith in the power of community education that we believe that, if by some magic all schools could be converted into broad based service centers, within a few generations, human suffering and despair could virtually be eliminated from the face of the earth. (p. xxv)

LeTarte and Minzey (1972) expressed a similar faith in the power of community education when they indicated:

The decision as to which direction education takes — which road we follow — will be made by that small group of dedicated people who believe in community education. They will make the decision to work like they have never worked before and they will accomplish the lofty goals community education can reach. (pp. 274-275)

In a tribute to the late Frank Manley, Melby (1972) stated:

No other educational leader in his period effected as complete a mobilization of community resources in a program to educate the entire community. No other educator has envisioned and set into universal operation, in his leadership area, a program that has so much promise of producing the new education without which the American Dream will falter. (p. 172)

Seay (1974) reinforced faith in the power of community education when he wrote:

> When in trouble, the American people have traditionally turned to education . . . It is the community education concept with its principle of basing learning upon problem solving that can satisfy the public demand for *help*. (p. 10)

However fervently expressed, commitment alone does not insure the resolution of the critical social problems facing either the developed or the developing nations of the world. *Leadership is required — leadership not only committed to making the world a better place for mankind but leadership capable of conceptualizing the interrelationships among the elements which comprise community, and leadership trained in the skills required to operationalize the tenets of the community education faith.*

COMMITMENT PLUS LEADERSHIP REQUIRED

In a publication entitled *Foundation for Living* (1977), the Charles Stewart Mott Foundation sets forth its future mission and the principles of governance required to implement that mission. The mission includes four prime thrusts aimed at enriching the lives of individuals and the community:

1. Opportunity for the Individual
2. Partnership with the Community
3. Effective Functioning of Community Systems
4. Leadership As the Mobilizer

William White, President of the Mott Foundation, speaking to the management guidelines accompanying the four thrusts above, pointed out that such guidelines are interrelated and that failure of any one of the parts can lead to failure of the whole. Similarly, it would seem that success in achieving any of the first three missions above depends to a great extent upon the fourth, namely, *leadership*. In the absence of leadership, opportunity for the individual to develop a partnership with his/her community cannot be assured nor can proper functioning of community systems be guaranteed.

The continued demand for leadership in community education in the years immediately ahead is virtually assured. Not only is there likely to be continued demand for leadership at the local level, there are increasing leadership opportunities at regional and state levels. Seven states have enacted legislation providing financial support for the establishing of local community education programs. Federal legislation provides funds for local experimental programs and staff for state departments of education. Also, the Mott Foundation continues to provide financial incentives to local schools, colleges, universities and state departments of education to establish centers for implementation, dissemination and training in community education. Whereas declining enrollments and dwindling funds forebode fewer job opportunities in education generally during the next decade, interest in extending educational opportunity to all community members and commitment to the empowerment of local leadership to resolve community problems are cause for optimism regarding leadership opportunities in the field of community education in the immediate future.

Those who aspire to positions of leadership in community education are well advised to examine the nature of the leadership requirements in the next decade and to prepare themselves, both personally and professionally, for such leadership roles. Inasmuch as leadership styles and skills in community education are discussed elsewhere in this publication, no attempt will be made to specify style or skill requirements. There are, however, a number of indicators of leadership emphases for the future which will be discussed briefly to provide direction to those preparing for future leadership roles.

INDICATORS OF FUTURE LEADERSHIP REQUIREMENTS

Whereas predictions regarding specific future leadership needs in community education can be misleading, there are indicators within the community education movement itself and within the society generally which provide direction for aspirants to future leadership positions within the movement. Indicators regarding future leadership needs within community education include:

1. *Cognizance among professional community educators of the necessity of both theory and practice to successful community leadership.*

The fact that no movement, however enthusiastically endorsed, is likely to survive without periodic examination of the assumptions upon which it is based is accepted by most professional educators today. The systematic examination of the assumptions underlying one's beliefs about a particular phenomenon and the development of testable hypotheses resulting from that examination involves basic theory development. Such an exercise is an essential part of the professional development of the aspiring community educator. Boles and Seay (1974) indicated:

Many people seem to believe that theory is a worthless academic exercise, of no use to practitioners in the field. Nothing could be further from the truth. John Dewey once said, "There is nothing so practical as a good theory." The great advances in the sciences and in technology have resulted from theory development. Advances in community education must also result from theory development. (p. 85)

Although attention to theory development is essential to success of the leader in community education, the testing of the theory in the community is of equal importance. It is only by testing the theory in a real life setting that one can judge the worth of either the theory or the practice.

Aspiring community educators are urged to develop a systematic framework of their beliefs about community education as a basis for their leadership in the community. In a society characterized by conflict and ambiguity, it is essential that the leader have a clear direction regarding the goal toward which he/she leads and a clear understanding of the consequences resulting from such direction. The process of theory development contributes to clarifying both the goal and the processes which contribute to reaching it.

Material included in this publication under Part I, "The Concept of Community Education," is intended to assist the leader in the process of clarifying the concept and in developing a theoretical framework from which to provide leadership to the community.

2. *Concern for the quality of life in the community — especially in urban areas.*

That the quality of life in the community is directly related to the success of the educational enterprise hardly requires documentation. The literature of the past decade is replete with evidence to support the contention that if the education process is to be successful it must take account of the social and economic factors impinging upon the learner. Acknowledging such evidence, many community educators have shared in the responsibility for improving the quality of life in their communities. Olsen (1977) points out:

> Some years ago, the *Study Commission on Undergraduate Education and the Education of Teachers* adopted a value statement which emphasized the importance of education to the formation of decent communities and the destructive effects of education which did not attend to the community formation process.

Olsen further illustrates the intervention of education institutions in the community improvement process by citing paradigms from several communities both rural and urban.

Past reports of successful community education intervention models come primarily from rural and suburban areas. However, there seems little doubt that the greatest challenge to community educators in the next decade will be somehow to impact the quality of life in large urban centers; for it is here that the consequences of failure to resolve social and economic problems pose the greatest threat to the entire society.

Such a challenge forces community educators to develop those skills required to provide leadership in the processes of community involvement and empowerment. The need for such skills may involve retraining for many of those already engaged in community education. The material included in this publication in Part II, "The Community Educator," examines the traits, skills and styles appropriate to the community leader of the future.

3. *Acceptance of the fact that "neighborhood" and "community" are no longer synonymous as they apply to many areas within the developed countries of the world.*

Totten and Manley recommended the neighborhood school as the delivery point for community educational services in 1969. In 1977, LeTarte and Minzey reiterated the viability of the school as the focal point for community education services:

The location of school buildings is normally ideal, in that they are built to serve population clusters. Few people are beyond walking distance of an elementary school. Opportunities in a neighborhood are much more appealing than a drive of some distance. (p. 30)

Granted that there are still many areas of America and other developed countries which look to the school as the locus of community services, there are a growing number of areas in which people seek "community" outside the local neighborhood. Mobility is a fact of life for most Americans. Increasingly for Americans and their counterparts throughout the world the church, the work place and the social group are not confined to the local neighborhood. Hence, leaders wishing to capitalize upon existing communities of interest must look outside the local neighborhood for their service areas and may no longer find the neighborhood school a viable center for community activity.

It is imperative that prospective community education leaders examine the nature of "community" in present-day society if their leadership efforts are to be properly directed. In Part III, "The Arena in Which Community Education is Practiced," this publication provides an analysis of the possible dichotomy between neighborhood and community, the use of social systems as they operate within the society and the political ramifications of leadership in the community context.

4. *Recognition that success for community leaders may depend more upon making the school a part of the community than upon getting the community to come to the school.*

Early in the community education movement emphasis was upon opening the school facilities to public use and promoting programs which brought the public to the school. The climactic moment in an early motion picture on community education, "To Touch a Child," was the point at which the school doors opened and the public of all ages surged into the school building to participate in school sponsored activities. By inference, success was measured by the numbers of people using the school building.

No doubt, community educators of the future will continue to promote use of the school facilities by the community. However, indications are that the emphasis of the future will be upon providing leadership to community groups and agencies in the process of attacking social and educational problems *in the community.* The locus of such leadership is likely to be the community, not the school.

That such leadership will require strategies quite different from those required to provide programs within the school seems obvious. Kimbrough (1977) indicated the direction of the training required to develop those strategies as follows:

> Central to the developing concept of community education is that educators must furnish leadership for the education of all people in concert with the leaders of other institutions of the society. Knowledge of the institutional structures of communities is important in assuming this leadership role. Educators need to become scholarly observers of the culture and the social structure of the communities in which they practice. (p. 25)

This publication discusses specific strategies for community leadership in Part IV, "Strategies for Community Education Leadership."

5. *Awareness that models projected to serve future community needs are likely to emphasize process over program.*

In tracing the history of the community education movement in this country, LeTarte and Minzey (1977) allude to a new role for community educators, namely, the *process* role:

> Building on the community school concept that had emerged, community education began to expand beyond its programmatic confines to a second stage which became known as process. This new view . . . built in a new emphasis — that of involving community residents in a close working relationship with existing institutions and agencies to combine forces in attacking community problems. (p. 28)

One hundred fifty doctoral and post-doctoral students participating in the Flint Laboratory for Intensive National Training sponsored by Western Michigan University over a three-year period generated theoretical models of community education with particular emphasis upon future directions.

Most of those models are based upon the same premise as that expressed by LeTarte and Minzey, namely, that the needs of the future demand processes aimed at community involvement and empowerment to resolve social and educational problems of the community. The following statements are typical of those accompanying the models developed by the community education scholars and serve to illustrate the process emphasis which they predict for the future:

Leadership can and should be developed from within the community.

The goal of community education is a heightened community awareness, identity, pride and capability.

Community education has the potential to bridge the communication gap between generations, cultures, races and/or religions.

Extensive involvement by the people served by the institution results in the institution better serving the people's needs.

The process of community education creates a communication system which promotes interaction at both personal and agency levels.

Community improvement has two dimensions — the personal growth of individuals and more effective interaction of those individuals with the community.

Success of community education can be measured in terms of the extent of community involvement in participative decision-making.

Problems belong to a community and not to an agency; when community members recognize that problems belong to them, they will be committed to program planning, problem solving and accountability.

If community is to enhance opportunities for the development of the individual and the individual is to improve the community, emphasis must be upon the strategies which relate the individual to his/her community.

The community educator is the spark which ignites community processes.

A body of people (community) benefits the extent to which each gives to the other.

Processes by which the community educator may provide leadership to his community are discussed in the section of this publication called Part IV, "Strategies for Community Education Leadership."

6. *Recognition by prospective community educators that the future of the profession is likely to be affected by developments at the regional, state, national and international levels.*

During the past decade community education has become a national movement due primarily to three factors: (1) a Regional Center network established by the Mott Foundation to disseminate the concept and train leadership, (2) legislation enacted by a number of states to provide funding to support local programs, and (3) Federal legislation establishing positions in state departments of education and stimulating innovation in local school districts throughout the nation. Such efforts have resulted in an expanded job market for community education leaders and new criteria for selection of prospective leaders in the movement. Further, the national network has resulted in the development of new models of community education and the sharing of results from the testing of new models and approaches by professional community educators.

There are indications that community education models are now being developed in a number of areas outside the United States — Australia, Canada, England, and South America to name a few. When the results of the testing of models in cultural settings outside the United States can be shared with community educators in this country, such information could profoundly alter both theory and practice.

Recent developments, both nationally and internationally, are cited in this publication in Part V, "The National Network for Promotion of Community Education."

It is to be hoped that future generations of leaders in community education will have the same commitment to improving the quality of life in their communities as did their predecessors. It is further to be hoped that the future leaders will be trained and retrained in those skills required to provide leadership in communities which are increasingly more complicated and constantly changing. This book addresses some of the issues with which prospective leaders must cope as they prepare themselves for the most important role in the field of community education — leadership capable of mobilizing the community for action.

REFERENCES

Boles, H., & Seay, M. In M. Seay, *Community education — a developing concept.* Midland, Mich.: Pendell Publishing Co., 1974.

Kimbrough, R. B. Community education implications for collegiate teacher educators. *Journal of Teacher Education,* July-August 1977.

LeTarte, C., & Minzey, J. *Community education: from program to process.* Midland, Mich.: Pendell Publishing Co., 1972.

LeTarte, C., & Minzey, J. Community education — where to now? *Journal of Teacher Education,* July-August 1977.

Melby, E. A salute to Frank J. Manley. *Phi Delta Kappan,* November 1972, p. 172.

Mott Foundation. *Foundation for living.* Flint, Mich.: Charles Stewart Mott Foundation, 1977.

Olsen, P. Community education — effects on local and world communities. *Journal of Teacher Education,* July-August 1977.

Seay, M. *Community education — a developing concept.* Midland, Mich.: Pendell Publishing Co., 1974.

Totten, F., & Manley, F. *The community school.* Galien, Mich.: Allied Education Council, 1969.

"The ultimate hope of the community educator is that all systems participating in any form of educational endeavor will willingly and continuously relate to the larger community educational picture and will participate openly in multi-systems planning, decision-making, and implementing." — *Wood*

Chapter 2

Operationalizing Community Education — The Open Systems Concept

by

George S. Wood, Jr.

OPERATIONALIZING COMMUNITY EDUCATION — THE OPEN SYSTEMS CONCEPT

INTRODUCTION

This study is an effort to examine the elements of community education and discover the fundamental principles on which implementation can be or should be based. The conclusions are that community education is characterized by the actions of a community's systems, that those systems must adopt operational modes consistent with the level of community education that is being implemented, and that these alternative operational levels and modes can be described in terms of different conditions of system *openness*.

The community education concept to be described in this discussion grows out of some fundamental assumptions:

1. Education is a lifelong process, and, therefore, the individual's *need for educational assistance* is lifelong. The need is no less important at age 40 than at age 14, although the goals, pattern, level, and extent of assistance may differ.
2. The potential for educational development, including basic academic and vocational skills development, in the individual is increased if the classroom is extended into the community and the community into the classroom.
3. People identify more readily with educational processes and are more motivated to support those when they are involved in determining directions for those processes.
4. Community people have a right to participate in decisions about the use of their public educational resources (and social/recreational resources, for that matter) and to expect those resources to be at their service optimally.
5. The citizens in any community can and will participate effectively in making decisions for the community when they are provided with the information that they need in each decision-making situation.
6. Every public situation/event has an educational element underlying its development and implied in its social effects. Therefore, each situation/event may be affected through educational processes and has educational effects of its own.
7. Virtually every institution, agency, and organization in a community functions to some extent in an educational role, although in many cases the role is neither clearly defined nor formally pursued.

8. Some educational tasks and/or some social problems cannot be addressed effectively by a single educational/social agent, but instead require the efforts of multiple agents acting in a coordinated manner.
9. In any community, an increased "sense of community" leads to greater educational efficiency and productivity. That is, the optimum use of educational resources increases the "sense of community" which in turn leads to more support for educational resource usage.
10. Whether a process or the result of a process, "education" refers to the teaching-learning that goes on among people, and, therefore, education occurs every moment of the day in every corner of the community — in formal classes, apprenticeships, real-life problems being solved, advice being given, examples being set, human relationships being worked out, and so forth.

Given these assumptions, community education, as an operational concept, is the teaching-learning which occurs through the actions of a community's *systems,* that is, institutions, organizations, and other formalized groups, which are the community's instruments for developing and administering the formal classes, apprenticeships, problem-solving efforts, formal advising, and planned human interactions, which constitute much of the educational experience of people. Community education is neither as broad as to include every instance of human learning experience in the community, nor as narrow as to be limited to the activities of any one community system. Instead, the term refers to those individual and community learning experiences which relate directly to the functioning of community systems aligned in varying combinations.

The nature and activity of these systems is the basic determinant of what might be called the *educational climate* in the community. These systems include, among others, school systems, (public and private), parks and recreation systems, social agencies and organizations, businesses, labor organizations, political and governmental systems, and so on. The term *educational climate* includes not only the numbers of learning opportunities available, but also the relevancy of those opportunities, the access of people to those opportunities and the general attitude of the people to both the opportunities and the deliverers or processors of those opportunities. A community in which these systems consistently process *sufficient, relevant, accessible* opportunities to a *receptive* population is well on the road to becoming what some people have called *the learning society* or what the Ball State Institute for Community Education Development staff refers to as the *fully functioning community.* The route to a fully functioning community is the development of a fully functioning community education process. A fully functioning community is one in which lifelong learning is a dominant ethic; the total community is the learning environment; the development of an effective, responsible citizenship is the goal; the development of a coordinated responsiveness of community service systems is the key strategy; and people involvement in participatory decision-making is the central feature.

In creating comprehensiveness, relevancy, accessibility, and public confidence, the essence of a community education effort which moves toward the *learning society* appears to be the development of systems which become increasingly open, that is, have more and more direct interaction with the community, both with the people and with other systems. The notion is that broad-based relevance and accessibility and public confidence in the systems are related to the degree of openness of those systems, individually and collectively. It is important for systems leaders to understand this notion because in implementing a more extensive community education approach, the issue is *not* simply whether to expand service/program dimensions, but whether to alter the fundamental nature of the systems in the direction of more *openness*.

THE SCHOOL AS AN EXAMPLE OF SYSTEM OPENNESS

The *openness* concept can be illustrated by an examination of the major areas of program activity in a comprehensive local school system community education effort. Although there may be some disagreement about terminology, most community educators would agree that the potential community school program focuses include the following: K-12 schooling for youth; K-12 schooling for adults (adult basic education and high school completion); K-12 experiences for early childhood; recreation; avocational, social and cultural activities; sub-community or neighborhood problems; and community-wide problems. (The term *K-12* refers to *kindergarten through twelfth grade,* but is meant to include post *12th grade* academic and vocational learning as well, wherever appropriate.) (See Figure 2-1.)

Figure 2-1

POTENTIAL LOCAL PROGRAM FOCUSES

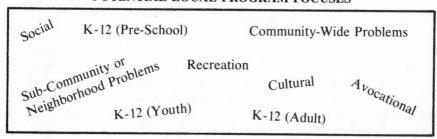

These nine focuses, from a local school system point of view, can be summed up in four different major operational or program dimensions: (1) K-12 schooling (youth); (2) extended K-12 schooling (adult and early childhood); (3) leisure education (avocational, social, cultural, and recreational); and (4) community problem solving (neighborhood and community-wide). Each of the four operational dimensions represents a major difference for the system in terms of the population to be served or service to be performed or process to be adopted. Starting with K-12 schooling as the basic, narrowest possible focus for the system, each succeeding dimension commits the system to a broader, more open-ended kind of interaction with the community. That is, the system itself has to become more *open* in order to function effectively in each succeeding operational arena.

Figure 2-2 puts these different dimensions into a pyramid to illustrate this increasing *openness*.

LEVELS OF SYSTEM OPENNESS IN SCHOOLS

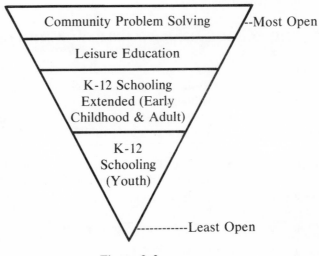

Figure 2-2

Community Problem Solving (Level 4) is an extremely complex category. Community problem solving refers to the kind of educational activity required to deal with such matters as environmental usage, energy usage, the aging process, public housing, public health, vandalism, neighborhood problems, and so forth. Operationally, a system may approach community problem solving on at least two different bases: (1) as an action area where the system determines its involvement behavior or (2) as a commitment by the system to a community process and community decision-making. The two

20

approaches require fundamentally different levels of system openness. The notion is that a system may be willing to operationalize one, but not the other. Therefore, a fifth level must be added, as in Figure 2-3.

EXTENDED LEVELS OF SYSTEM OPENNESS

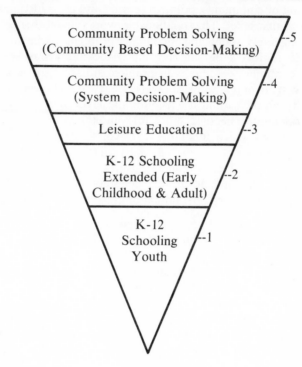

Figure 2-3

Level 5 (Community Problem Solving — Community Based Decision-Making) may also be described as a *Community Based Operation* or *Community Based Community Education*. The Level 5 assumption is that education is ultimately a function of the community and that the role(s) and location(s) of system activity, even those that are traditional, are subject to community definition and redefinition. There is also a further implication that at this level the system voluntarily participates in and becomes subject to community-based decision-making and planned coordination.

Further Levels Relationships

The reader should be aware that the pyramid levels have a collective quality about them. That is, each level presumes the inclusion of the activities in the levels below it. With respect to *community problem solving,* for example, to the extent that the academic needs of youth, adult education needs, early childhood education needs, leisure time learning needs, career learning needs, environmental learning needs, social learning needs, political learning needs, and the learning requirements for the solutions to individual and group problems are all situations about which the community must do something, then all of these categories of learning activity fall under the general heading of community problem solving and are addressed by a system working at that level. This relationship works in another way, also. If the system completely adopts the community problem solving mode of operation necessary for levels four and five, it then inevitably must see an interrelationship of community elements in problem situations. The system then begins to view its own operation at levels one, two, and three in the light of the community problems that it encounters at level four or five. Thus, the lower level operations become more relevant to the broader community situation. A system which functions at Level 4 openness can (and does) fulfill its responsibilities of Levels 1, 2, and 3. In fact, it probably does so in a more creative and productive manner. But a system which functions at Level 2 openness cannot (and usually does not) address Level 4 responsibilities with any degree of operational optimism.

The five levels have not been presented as "Five Stages of Community Education Development," although they may be viewed by some in that light. Certainly a long range plan to reach Level 5 which is implemented by advancing from level to level is an appropriate strategy. However, the movement from level to level is by no means a "natural" or "logical" expectation for any system. The different requirements of system openness at each level mean new commitments for a system which moves from one level to another, commitments which the system may be unwilling to make, no matter how successful it has been at the lesser degree of openness.

The System Must Decide

What happens, of course, is that the school system decides which levels or focuses will be included in its local community education effort. In determining the composite focuses of its implementation, the system is defining its mission or role in the community and, consequently, the level of openness on which it "intends" to operate. However, *openness* consists of more than specified intentions. *Openness* involves at least the communication, planning, decision-making, and resource allocation patterns of the system. The idea is that if the system intends to function effectively in the focus areas that it specifies as its mission, then it must adopt communication, planning, decision-making, and resource allocation procedures which can support the system's efforts in those areas. The resulting condition is a particular level of *operational openness*. As the mission changes in dimension, the degree or level of openness of the system itself changes toward greater or lesser openness.

Several implications are evident here. Sometimes the mission of the system is determined less by what is appropriate for the community than by the degree of openness that system leaders can "tolerate" in their personal and professional behavior styles. Sometimes the system mission is determined on the basis of community needs, but the system fails to recognize the importance of adopting the *openness* characteristics necessary to support the mission. Sometimes well-meaning community education advocates promote the idea that the concept is simply a "program expansion" notion which does not require fundamental change by the system, but only some "additional" resources or activities. The reader can undoubtedly add other implications.

The singular factor then which identifies the relative condition of the system's community education effort at any given moment is system *openness*. The key indicators for fixing the degree of system openness are its role assumptions, its communication patterns, its planning procedures, and its resource allocation procedures. The reader should be cautioned that temporary and/or exceptional activity in any one of these indicator areas can produce inaccurate conclusions about system openness, if the exceptional indicator condition is the only factor considered. The fact that a system, by virtue of incidental circumstance or temporary credibility requirements, may be able to point to programs or services or isolated people involvement actions does not mean that the system is operating at the level of openness which is apparent in those actions. The entire system operation must be examined. Operating assumptions must be identified and tested. Communications and decision-making patterns must be checked out. The isolated actions must be found to be consistent with the fundamental operational mode of the system.

Openness Levels Are Relative and Applicable to Other Systems

The reader should understand that degrees or levels of "openness" are relative concepts. The five levels identified in this study are not absolutes. The reader should imagine a continuum of openness with the five levels being arbitrary points along the continuum which are definable in terms of their differences from each other. In the social setting, there is no completely closed or completely open system. Being completely closed would exclude the system from any contact with the society, and being completely open would obliterate any consistent characteristics by which a system could be identified at all.

In the same way that schools can be seen as *opening,* so do other agencies and organizations open as they participate in the community education process. Each system can be described in community education terms as operating at a *level of openness* on the following 5-level pyramid in Figure 2-4:

DESCRIPTIONS OF LEVELS OF SYSTEM OPENNESS

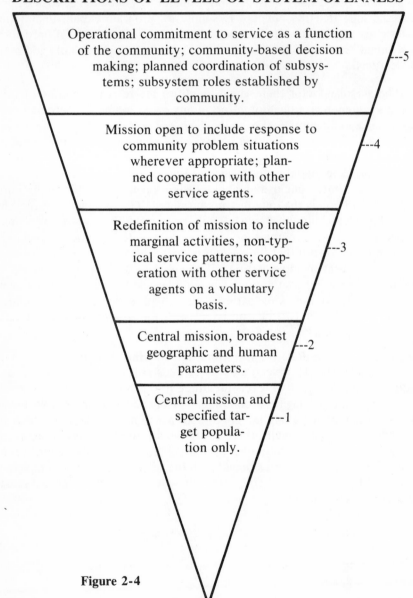

Operational commitment to service as a function of the community; community-based decision making; planned coordination of subsystems; subsystem roles established by community. ---5

Mission open to include response to community problem situations wherever appropriate; planned cooperation with other service agents. ---4

Redefinition of mission to include marginal activities, non-typical service patterns; cooperation with other service agents on a voluntary basis. ---3

Central mission, broadest geographic and human parameters. ---2

Central mission and specified target population only. ---1

Figure 2-4

The school system pyramid previously described is a specific example of this general systems pyramid. The contention here is that similar specific pyramids can and should be developed for recreation departments, social agencies, and other systems.

MULTI-SYSTEM OPENNESS = "COMMUNITY" EDUCATION

If the relative condition of a system's community education activity is determined by that system's openness, then the nature of an entire community's condition is determined by the openness of its many systems acting in concert. The functions of individual systems can best be described by the phrase *participation in,* as in "school system participation in community education" or "the parks and recreation department participation in community education." The question for each system is how broadly and how intensively it will "participate in" community education, that is, how relatively "open" its operation will be. *Community* education refers to the conditions and processes which result from the multi-system interaction pattern. The pattern in turn is determined by the openness of the individual systems.

Cooperation and co-ordination among systems comes from their operating at a level of openness which structures the necessary interaction as logical operating procedure. Given the *openness* necessary in the operating systems, what remains to be done is the structuring of operational mechanisms (mutually agreed upon patterns or processes for initiating and maintaining ongoing interaction among the systems). Again, the key to this coordination dimension of the concept lies in the conscious *structuring of appropriate mechanisms* consistent with openness characteristics of the various systems involved. Although cooperation in any form or for whatever reason is ordinarily commendable, the principle being examined here is *not* found in cooperation efforts, incidental or on-going, whose purpose is to comply with externally imposed sanctions or legal requirements or funding guidelines. Nor is the principle at work when the cooperation is the result of informal personal relationships developed by middle management people in the various systems to accomplish what the systems themselves can't do formally. The principle being described refers to a system level of openness and cooperative relationships which result from a consciously planned, fundamental operational mode for the system(s). In arguing that the proper procedure for developing a cooperative community education climate is first to open each system and then develop *interaction mechanisms,* the writer is aware that the process is not as orderly or as clearcut as the argument suggests. Actually, the mechanisms are developed *as the systems open.* However, the point is that a mechanism can't be expected to work if the systems are not *open* enough to participate at the level necessary for the mechanism to function productively.

What is being suggested here is that a system's purposes for structuring cooperation/coordination (its organizational mental set) are typically different at each level. Similarly, its purposes for structuring citizen involvement are fundamentally different at each level. Clearly, systems operating at different levels of openness may find themselves at "cross-purposes" when they attempt to cooperate, particularly if some joint effort at citizen involvement is part of the cooperative project. Figure 5 charts each level of system openness in terms of the system mission and target population, the individual system commitment required, the typical function of community council or citizen involvement, the typical functions of multi-system cooperation/coordination, and the typical function of each system.

During the early years in the development of the community education concept across the country (at least until the middle 1970's) the focus has largely been on *opening up* the school system in each community. It has been a *community schools* effort to increase the school system's *participation in community education.* The school system is a very important system, but only one of the many systems that affect the educational climate in any community. The *multi-system* approach is still largely untried. For this reason, the process for increasing cooperation among systems has often been one of creating a "mechanism" arbitrarily for the interaction (an agency council created by the schools, for example) and then trying to persuade systems to participate in the mechanism, without regard to the levels of operational openness in the systems or the type of mechanism which would best accommodate the operating conditions of the particular systems in question.

THE ULTIMATE HOPE

Community education addresses the interrelationship, even the interdependence of public schooling, adult education, early childhood education, leisure education, community problem solving, and community development in a community educational pattern. It doesn't address any component so much from a programmatic point-of-view as from the matter of its place in the total educational pattern of the community. The question is whether the community's educational patterns are effectively addressing the community's complex problems or needs.

If recreators and public school people, for example, really believe in community education, they believe not only that cooperative programming and sharing facilities and resources make economic and public relations sense, but also that their educational missions are inevitably related, that they are dependent upon one another in an educational sense. The assumption is that the educational process is really aiming at helping people to

TYPICAL ORGANIZATIONAL BEHAVIOR AT THE MULTI-SYSTEMS LEVELS

Level	System Mission & Target Population	Individual System Operational Commitment	Function of Council or Community Involvement Mechanisms	Primary Cooperation/Coordination Functions	Operational Function of each system
1	Central/traditional mission specified target population by age, location, ethnic or social affiliation	To function within its primary charter mandate; to limit its services and use of resources to the primary area of responsibility only.	Single system councils or mechanisms to review system plans and performance and provide reactive input from the community.	To establish distinct and separate service responsibilities and territories for each system.	To make all decisions for system action; to create all administrative processes for implementing decisions.
2	Central/traditional mission; Target population expanded to include segments not included at Level 1, sometimes the entire community.	To make the traditional services of the system available to the widest possible segment of the population.	Single system councils or mechanisms to provide reactive program input and to provide contact with client populations.	To share basic information about the mission of each system; to minimize duplication.	To make all decisions for system action; to create all administrative processes for implementing decisions; to structure some community input into planning.
3	Redefinition of Mission to include marginal activities, non-traditional service patterns; target population the entire community being served.	To make the widest possible effective use of system resources in serving the community.	Single and/or multi-systems mechanisms to provide general input for mission definition; to identify service deficiencies; to motivate multi-system interaction.	To share continuous information about mission emphases; to share experiences, techniques, and materials where missions of different systems have common elements; to control duplication	To make all decisions for system action; to structure some sharing with other systems in designing administrative processes; to structure regular/substantial community involvement in planning.
4	Mission open to include response to community problem situation wherever appropriate; target population defined by problem situations but open to include all community people potentially.	To function in a problem solving role; to participate in problem areas that are seen by system leadership as consistent with the systems priorities and resources.	Multi-systems mechanisms to identify community problem areas and priorities for consideration by the systems; to assume other support, planning, and implementation roles as defined by the systems.	To process problem definition and planning among systems; to mobilize sets of multi-system resources required to address problems; to create action guidelines for each system to observe on voluntary basis.	To accept community decisions as action parameters; to decide which problem/need areas the system will actively address; to create administrative & implementation processes consistent with joint cooperative/coordinative planning decisions or guidelines.
5	Mission to serve as a function of community in completely open-ended community decision-making setting; target population same as Level 4.	To function as an instrument of the community on a peer level with all other systems; to be subject to decisions made by the community through its multi-system operational process.	Multi-systems mechanisms to identify problems, establish priorities, and make decision about necessary community action outcomes which become binding upon the system actions; to assume other planning and implementation responsibilities as determined by the problem setting and the citizen potential.	To process problem definition and multi-systems decision-making governing; to mobilize sets of multi-system resources in each problem area; to assign individual system tasks, which become binding upon those systems; to create inter-system administrative procedures for each problem area.	To create administrative and implementation processes to address the tasks assigned by the community, consistent with the multi-system planning decisions.

Figure 2-5

improve their self-images, helping them to learn to adjust to change, helping them to create meaningful social patterns and relationships, helping them to make better use of the environment, etc. It is unrealistic to assume that such matters as personal self-image, the aging process, peer social relationships, social change adjustment, or effective environmental usage, either at the individual level or the community level, can be addressed by agencies acting unilaterally or in a loose programmatic alliance posture, where the main function of the alliance is to divide up the service pie and make sure that each agent doesn't interfere with the other's territory. Possibly one of the reasons that community education as a concept has been threatening to a good many people, including scores of public school people, is that in its broadest conceptual form, it says, "The old notion of territory is out-moded. It doesn't provide a basis for getting at the real socio-educational questions which confront us." The needs are not simple, but complex. Most community problems require the joint action of many community systems in differing combinations. Sets of resources must go where the need is and in whatever form that the need requires. Although it is important to have service systems of people with special skills, these systems must be less concerned about maintaining an exclusive organizational structure and territory and more concerned about adapting to the need requirements. Each system must realize that even its narrowest, most parochial actions do have an impact, positive or negative, upon the broader community and its many problem situations. Likewise, the actions of other systems have an impact upon even the most unique community service situations of any individual system. Somehow there has to be created a consistent and effective process of multi-system decision-making and interaction to deal with education as the complex process that it is.

The ultimate hope of the community educator is that all systems participating in any form of educational endeavor will willingly and continuously relate to the larger community educational picture and will participate openly in multi-systems planning, decision-making, and implementing. The process of multi-system resource interaction, planning, and decision-making which results in a community problem solving orientation for education is the focus of community education as practiced in its most conceptually-advanced form. Community education then is community development in an educational sense or with *education of some kind* seen as the cornerstone of, and an ingredient in, all developmental community activity. It is a way of looking at education as multi-faceted, multi-system, interrelated sets of activities designed to produce some specific problem solutions and to promote the interactive pattern of community problem solving.

THE DIRECTOR OR COORDINATOR

The visible community education administrative structure for the multi-systems model becomes whatever administrative pattern functions best in the given community and is consistent with the level of community education activity being implemented. Whether the processes and programs and resources are physically managed by someone formally titled "The Community Education Director" or other people is not the real question. In fact, it can be argued that as a programmer, the Community Education Director really is a recreator or an adult educator or a social director, stepping in and out of those roles as the occasion demands. In that case, the role of such a programmer in leisure education or adult education is exactly the same as the people who are called *recreators* and *adult educators*. He/she plans, implements, and supervises activities as time and resources permit. He/she seeks cooperative relationships with the other agencies who are programming in the same areas and tries to avoid duplication or competition as much as possible. He/she usually has a Level 3 operation located in one agency and is a kind of jack-of-all-trades leader who does his/her thing. The net result too often is that community education establishes its own agency, which joins the other community bureaucracies competing for visibility, territory, and program funding.

If community education is really a systematic and purposeful mix of the community's educational forces, the community educator is not the expert or supervisor of any one of those forces, except as emergency requires such an action. Instead, community educators are motivators and facilitators for community problem analysis; for communication across geographic, social, and organizational lines; for developing multi-system educational action designs or master plans; and for optimizing the involvement of community people in making action decisions. He/she is the *advocate* of education as a complex, community problem solving force and the *servant* of community individuals and organizations who want to participate in implementing such a concept. Needless to say, training for these positions must be consistent with the roles and the level of implementation.

For purely economic or other practical reasons, the community education leader(s) may be housed in one community system or in a position jointly created by two or three systems. Or, for local political reasons there may be a need in some communities to create a *community* position, not directly tied to any single system. The intention here is not to argue the merits of alternative administrative structures.

Whatever the administrative pattern adopted, the kind of role that such people must play is clear. At least five role functions seem imperative: (1)

community ombudsman or advocate, (2) community process person, (3) trainer of other community process people, (4) community information gatherer and disseminator, and (5) evaluator-analyst-reporter-to-the-community on the condition of the *educational climate*. These role functions are to be contrasted with the other role such a person sometimes is expected to play, that of *community manipulator* for the system(s) which signs the paycheck. Parenthetically, this is to suggest that even where systems are interested only in better "public relations," they would do well to identify their community services or relations director as "the community's person on our premises" and then really encourage and support him/her in that role.

CONCLUSION

In the larger context, the community education leader has to be the community's person *on every system's premises*. And the real question which confronts communities who are moving in community education directions is not "Do we want another leisure education director or adult education director?" but instead "Do we want to operate with a master educational plan for the community?" At the same time, system leaders must ask themselves, "Do we want to commit our respective systems to interaction and interdependence patterns prescribed by the problems to be solved, rather than the traditional missions of the interacting systems? Are we willing to be coordinated in a decision-making process to which we contribute, but which our system does not unilaterally control?" The level of community education that a community can expect to actualize depends upon the answers.

With additional development and specification, the multi-systems concept has a number of potential uses. It can provide a framework for use by local systems in identifying their operational level of openness. It can be used for prescribing the basic system changes that are necessary if the system is to move from one level to another. It can be a tool for analyzing relationships between systems on the basis of their respective openness levels. It can be used in designing citizen involvement mechanisms and/or systems cooperation mechanisms. And it can be used as a basis for designing both local leadership job descriptions and relevant training for those local positions. This article and the many communities across the country have only begun to scratch the surface of the multi-systems concept. More investigation and application would seem to be called for.

REFERENCES

Buckley, Walter. *Sociology and modern systems theory.* Englewood Cliffs, New Jersey: Prentice-Hall, Inc., 1967.

Burian, William A., and Flynn, John P. *The systems approach as philosophy and framework for social work.* (Unpublished Manuscript) Kalamazoo, Michigan: Western Michigan University, 1974.

Decker, L. E. *Foundations of community education.* Midland, Michigan: The Pendell Company, 1972.

Decker, L. E. *People helping people.* Midland, Michigan: The Pendell Company, 1975.

Deutsch, Karl W. *The resolution of conflict.* New Haven: Yale University Press, 1973.

The fully functioning community (Unpublished handout). Institute For Community Education Development, Ball State University, 1975.

Hickey, H. W., and Van Voorhees, C. V. *The role of the school in community education.* Midland, Michigan: The Pendell Company, 1969.

Homans, George C. *The human group.* New York: Harcourt, Brace and World, Inc., 1950.

Irwin, Martha, and Russell, Wilma. *The community is the classroom.* Midland, Michigan: The Pendell Company, 1971.

Kariel, Henry S. *Open systems: arenas for political action.* Itasca, Illinois: F. A. Peacock Publishers, Inc., 1968.

Katz, D., and Kahn, R. L. *The social psychology of organizations.* New York: Wiley, 1966.

Kerensky, V. M., and Melby, E. O. *Education II: The social imperative.* Midland, Michigan: The Pendell Company, 1971.

Kuhn, Alfred. *The logic of social systems.* San Francisco: Jassey-Bass Publishers, 1974.

Minzey, Jack D., and LeTarte, Clyde E. *Community education: from program to process.* Midland, Michigan: The Pendell Company, 1972.

Monane, Joseph H. *A sociology of human systems.* New York: Appleton-Century-Crofts, 1967.

Saxe, Richard W. *School-community interaction.* Berkley, California: McCutchaw Publishing Corp., 1975.

Seay, Maurice F., and Crawford, Ferris N. *The community school and community self-improvement.* Lansing, Michigan: Clair L. Taylor, 1951.

Seay, Maurice F., and Associates. *Community education: a developing concept.* Midland, Michigan: The Pendell Company, 1974.

Totten, W. Fred, and Manley, Frank J. *The community school.* Galien, Michigan: Allied Education Council, 1969.

"It would appear that proponents of community education have a great deal of work to do in defining the uniqueness of the concept as it relates to the traditional day-school program. This task might best be accomplished by the development of a model day-school program which truly incorporates unique elements of the community education philosophy." — *Jeffrey*

Chapter 3

Staff Commitment and Success of the Community Education Process

by

John B. Jeffrey

STAFF COMMITMENT AND SUCCESS OF THE COMMUNITY EDUCATION PROCESS

Authorities have maintained for years that the teacher in a community education setting is a unique instructor. In 1939 Clapp outlined the role of the teacher in a community school:

A teacher who enters community education surrenders prerogatives. His authority is the authority not of position, but of usable knowledge confirmed by action and events. Community education is not brought into being by the putting over of a plan, or by the imposing of ideas. It requires that full recognition be given to people's desires and needs, feelings and opinions, ways of doing and thinking; and that the relation of any particular enterprise to other enterprises and to the whole be currently understood. The demands on anyone directing it is to recognize opportunities when they appear — usually unlabeled — and to use the capacities of everyone — including himself — at the time and in the way that will help the enterprise and the people in it; to discern new developments, fresh approaches to the problem, and different ways of getting past obstacles. (p. 170)

Seay, writing in 1945, indicated that the teacher in a community school played a vital role in improving the life of the community:

In addition to knowing children and the subject matter to be taught, teachers of schools which emphasize community resources and needs must know the interests and the customs of the people whom they serve, their problems, and how they make a living. They must know the organizations and methods of the other public services of the community. They must know how the problems of patrons and the agencies of the community relate to problems and agencies elsewhere in the state, in the nation, and in the world. Above all they must know how to study a local community so as to identify its problems and resources. (p. 226)

Muntyan (1953) listed a multiplicity of skills to be mastered by the community school teacher: (1) mastery of subject area; (2) ability to work with groups; (3) expertness in the application of philosophy, sociology, and the biological sciences as they underlie the educative process; (4) ability to help students evaluate themselves and the social process; and (5) an ability to understand and interpret the society in which they teach. Additionally, Muntyan mused that "the teacher must become at least a minor prophet, since he must, in a very real sense, predict the direction in which the community wants to move." (p. 44)

Recent literature, too, has speculated that the true community school dictates requirements for performance of teachers which are broader than, and different from the requirements of the traditional school. These requirements include (1) being aware of and using community resources on a regular basis, (2) demonstrating a willingness to study the community and view it as a laboratory for learning, (3) being aware that the classroom is only one of many educative processes in the community, (4) a willingness to share school and classroom facilities with others, and (5) acceptance of the potential of lay participation in the educational process (Keidel, 1969).

Minzey and Olsen (1969) maintained that in addition to placing new requirements for teacher performance, the philosophy demands a new role of the teachers:

> The role of the teacher in community education will differ from that of the teacher in the traditional setting. In addition to his responsibilities as a teacher, he will need to be informed and supportive of the existing programs. His knowledge of outside programs will help him to select the educational experiences of his students. He will need to develop an attitude toward community involvement that will foster and promote the basic ideas of community education. His role will represent a key position in the development of a sense of community in the students he teaches and the parents with whom he works. This role will consist of being involved in extra-school activities, both as a teacher and as a participant, and fostering professional and social activities which tend to bring his services more in contact with the community. Parent conferences, home visits, and community service will be integral parts of the teacher's role in community education. (p. 37)

Several authorities have held that the most important difference between the teacher in the traditional school and the teacher in the community school can be found in the attitude of the teacher. Kerensky and Melby (1971) held that the teacher in the community school possesses an unusual amount of faith in people. Community school teachers assume that people (particularly youngsters) can be trusted, want to be successful, and will be successful if given the opportunity. According to Whitt (1971), the teacher within a system of community education recognizes individual differences in children, believes all children can learn, and is concerned about the self-concept of the child. Finally, Hiemstra (1972) wrote that the community school teacher (1) relates what happens in the classroom to the home and community, (2) is willing to work with parents and students in supplemental educational activities in the home and community, and (3) is willing to visit homes to better determine and understand educational needs.

Further, recent literature has pointed out that the community education philosophy ascribes a different role for the teacher. Commenting upon this role, Campbell (1971) wrote that the traditional school was concerned about what the teacher *taught,* while the community school is concerned about what and how children *learn.* He continued to describe this role of the teacher by indicating that the teacher "should be a diagnostician, a prescriber, and an evaluator" (p. 32). Further, Campbell held that the teacher must realize that the student gets motivation from a great many different sources and that some lay people may be more successful than the teachers themselves in teaching youngsters certain things.

In spite of the lofty ideals expressed in the literature cited above, many community educators worried that teachers were not accepting this new role nor were they "buying" the community education philosophy. Hanna (1972) reported that analysis of case studies of abandoned community school efforts seem to point to "the lack of understanding of the goals (of community education) and inadequate or inappropriate content and method on the part of the teaching profession" (p. 17).

Kerensky and Melby (1971) contended that in order for community education to develop an open, positive learning atmosphere, the schools must have teachers with goals, methods, and attitudes which can produce the proper climate for learning. They warned that teachers who do not understand and accept the philosophy are often the major "roadblock" to its affecting the K-12 program:

> Many teachers see a community school as a mere addition to the usual K-12 program. It may be viewed as a good addition to the "regular" program. It is sometimes seen as a good program to be paid for by special funds. In many established "community schools," this inadequate perception prevails. The school is "lighted" and open in the evening. Interesting activities are conducted in the afternoon and evening, but the school for children during the day is untouched by the concept. (p. 182)

Keidel's (1969) comments also pointed to the importance of teacher understanding and acceptance of the philosophy. He wrote that teachers must be cognizant of, and willing to use, community resources in the classroom. Further, Keidel stressed that teachers must be aware of and accept the fact that the teacher is not the sole educational and social catalyst in a child's life and that the classroom is no longer the sole domain of the teacher. In short, the teacher must understand the concept and identify his role within it, if it is to affect the K-12 program.

An apparently frustrated Clark wrote that in many cases the K-12 program had not been affected:

> Probably the biggest frustration to active community educators today is the lack of acceptance of basic community education principles into the regular school day instructional programs. Many school systems across this nation have expanded their educational services by providing exciting after school, evening and summer learning experiences for community members of all ages. However, in most cases these same school systems continue to maintain very conventional and static regular school day programs oriented to "book learning." (Clark, 1974, p. 33)

Melby (1971), writing in the *Community Education Journal,* appeared to agree with Clark's assessment of the situation. He held that there is often too much of a separation between the evening program for adults and the day program for children. He added that teachers of the day program have little contact with the evening program and hence miss many opportunities to interact with parents of children they instruct during the day.

Again addressing himself to this problem, Melby (1971) expressed the frustration of many community educators when he questioned how a community school with a successful evening program could continue to produce drop-outs, children with poor self-images, and children with no saleable skills. He answered his own query by pointing out that there is a lack of acceptance on the part of teachers of basic tenets of the community education philosophy.

The literature referred to above provides an example of the conflicting ideas which have been expressed regarding teacher staff commitment to the community education concept. Some authorities have held that teachers within systems of community education are committed to a unique educational philosophy, perform a unique pedogogical role, maintain unique attitudes toward people, and encounter unique on-the-job performance requirements. Other authorities have held that the message of community education has not reached daytime K-12 teachers and that they neither understand nor accept the basic tenets of the community education philosophy.

In order to resolve this dilemma, the writer (Jeffrey, 1975) conducted research related to teacher acceptance of the community education philosophy. Specifically, the research compared teachers in districts with and without operative community education programs to determine the extent of differences in acceptance of the community education philosophy as a whole, six components of the philosophy (see Minzey, 1974) and program and process aspects of the philosophy.

The population sample used in the study was comprised of 258 teachers selected at random from over 5,700 teachers employed in 134 school districts in Southwest Michigan. The instrument utilized in the investigation was the Community Education Philosophy Instrument (CEPI), a 63-item questionnaire which measured the extent to which each statement reflected the respondent's personal educational philosophy. The data were analyzed by use of appropriate correlation coefficients and the t test for independent samples.

The results of the study revealed that there were differences in the extent of acceptance of the community education philosophy among instructional staff groups from districts with and without community education programs. In general, teachers from districts with programs in existence for at least 3 years showed greater acceptance of the philosophy than did teachers from districts without operative programs. These results appear to confirm the claims of Kerensky and Melby (1971), Whitt (1971), and Clark (1972) that teachers who are exposed to community education programs within their own school district tend to be more supportive of the concept.

It is important to note, however, that both teacher groups consistently demonstrated moderate to strong acceptance of the philosophy. Both groups indicated at least moderate acceptance of the philosophy as a whole, the six components of the philosophy, the program aspects of the philosophy, and the process aspects of the philosophy. This general acceptance of the philosophy by both instructional staff groups provided evidence that, in a geographic area well saturated with community education programs, most teachers are aware of the concept and, as a result of this awareness, tend to be more accepting of the concept.

The general findings of the study do not support the contention of Melby (1971) and others that there is a lack of acceptance on the part of teachers of the basic tenets of the philosophy. Quite to the contrary, responses to the CEPI revealed, among teachers in southwest Michigan, that there was moderate to strong acceptance of these basic tenets.

Additionally, study results indicated that proponents of community education in southwest Michigan need not fear, as did Kerensky and Melby (1971) and Hanna (1972), that a lack of teacher acceptance will hinder the development of community education programs. Indeed, the study revealed that at least a modicum of teacher acceptance exists even in those districts without programs. In short, it does not appear that a lack of teacher acceptance of the concept will be a roadblock to efforts to begin new programs.

Finally, it should be pointed out that the findings of this investigation do not lend credence to the argument of Minzey and LeTarte (1972) that the major difference between teachers in traditional schools and community schools can be found in their philosophies of education. Although the present study revealed greater acceptance of the philosophy on the part of community school teachers, it did not reveal that the two instructional staff groups espoused fundamentally different educational philosophies.

Perhaps the most surprising result of the study was that differences did *not* exist in teacher acceptance of items related to teaching in the traditional day-school program. Keidel (1969), Melby (1968), Hiemstra (1972), Irwin and Russell (1971), and others have steadfastly maintained that community school teachers are unique because they (1) advocate the use of community resources in the classroom, (2) view the community as a laboratory for learning, (3) bring the "community into the classroom" and the "classroom into the community," (4) understand that life experiences teach more than academic study, (5) show great concern for the self-concept of the child, and (6) adhere to other aspects of the community education philosophy. Quite to the contrary, the present study revealed that teachers from districts with *and* without community education programs demonstrated a high level of acceptance of items such as those listed above.

The results of the writer's research appear to have several important implications for the success of the community education concept and, more specifically for the relationship between community education and the K-12 instructional program.

Study results indicate that most teachers in an area saturated with community education programs are aware of and accepting of certain aspects of the philosophy. For example, when a school district adopts the concept, the change most apparent to the teacher is probably the extended usage of school and classroom facilities once thought to be the private domain of the "regular school" teacher. The results of the study indicated that teachers have accepted this change.

However, the community education philosophy as it relates to the traditional day-school program, appears to be a collection of rather general pedagogical principles which are espoused by most teachers whether or not they work within a system of community education. Hence, it would appear that proponents of community education have a great deal of work to do in defining the uniqueness of the concept as it relates to the traditional day-school program.

This task might best be accomplished by the development of a model day-school program which truly incorporates unique elements of the community education philosophy. Such a "radical" model would include such concepts as: moving students and teachers out from the "four walls" of the classroom into the larger classroom of the community; the development of a curriculum centered fully around the problems of the community; *extensive* community involvement in the K-12 instructional program; and full realization that the school is only a partner among the many educational agencies at work in the community. Careful evaluation of such a model would provide a "giant step" toward the goal of defining the uniqueness of the concept.

Another implication of the study is the important discovery that most teachers are not adversaries of the community education movement. In short, teachers (in southwest Michigan) proved to be accepting and supportive of the concept. As such, they represent a largely untapped resource to proponents of community education.

It would appear that there are a myriad of ways in which this resource could be taped in districts with community education programs. Teachers might serve on advisory councils; help identify and recruit students for adult basic education and high-school completion classes; provide a communication link with parents; verbalize support for the concept to community residents, board members, and school administrators; aid in the training of evening-program teachers; teach in the evening program; and share ideas and resources with the community education director.

In districts without community education programs, teacher support would be an invaluable resource in convincing community residents, board members, and school administrators of the value of the concept. Although K-12 teachers are not primary decision makers regarding the implementation of the concept at the local level, their enthusiasm for the concept would certainly have a positive impact upon board members and school administrators. In addition, their support of the concept would certainly be the chief determinant of the impact of the concept upon the traditional day-school program.

A final implication of the study relates to in-service training for teachers. Little in-service training related to community education had been provided for teachers included in the study. In spite of this scarcity of in-service efforts, most teachers in the study indicated at least a moderate level of acceptance of the concept. These results suggest that strong in-service efforts might increase teacher support of the concept.

Professional community educators should work together to develop in-service programs for instructional staffs. Attention should be directed to the efforts of educators who have already attempted to develop such programs. The in-service methodologies of these educators should be reviewed, evaluated, and collated into a training model which could be made available to interested individuals.

At the beginning of this chapter the writer presented several questions: are teachers within systems of community education committed to a unique educational philosophy; do these teachers accept a different and unique pedagogical role; do they maintain a different attitude toward students, adults, and the community; and do they encounter unique on-the-job performance requirements? The answer to the above questions is probably not. However, study results indicated that teachers in both community education and non-community education settings showed at least moderate acceptance of the community education philosophy. In short, the seeds of solid teacher acceptance of the concept have been sown. The task for today's professional community educator is to see that the philosophy, as it relates to the day-school program, is clarified so that these seeds can germinate.

REFERENCES

Campbell, C. M. Community education — America's hope for the future. *Community Education Journal,* 1971, *1* (3), 32-37.

Clapp, E. R. *Community schools in action.* New York: Viking Press, 1939.

Clark, P. A. Guidelines for relating community education and the regular school instructional program. *Community Education Journal,* 1972, *2* (1), 60-62.

Clark, P. A. Can basic community education principles be included in the K-12 program? *Community Education Journal,* 1974, *4* (1), 33-35.

Hanna, P. R. What thwarts the community school curriculum? *Community Education Journal,* 1972, *2* (3), 15-17.

Hiemstra, R. *The educative community.* Lincoln, Neb.: Professional Educators Publications, 1972.

Irwin, M., & Russell, W. *The community is the classroom.* Midland, Mich.: Pendell Publishing, 1971.

Jeffrey, J. B. *A comparative study of teacher acceptance of the community education philosophy in southwest Michigan.* Unpublished doctoral dissertation, Western Michigan University, 1975.

Keidel, G. E. Staffing and training. In H. W. Hickey & C. Van Voorhees (Eds.), *The role of the school in community education.* Midland, Mich.: Pendell Publishing, 1969.

Kerensky, V. M., & Melby, E. O. *Education II: The social imperative.* Midland, Mich.: Pendell Publishing, 1971.

Melby, E. O. The community school: A social imperative. *The Community School and Its Administration,* 1968, *7* (2), 2-3.

Melby, E. O. Lighting the schoolhouse at night is not enough. *Community Education Journal,* 1971, *1* (2), 4.

Minzey, J. D. Community education — Another perception. *Community Education Journal,* 1974, *4* (3), 7; 58-61.

Minzey, J. D., & LeTarte, C. E. *Community education: From program to process.* Midland, Mich.: Pendell Publishing, 1972.

Minzey, J. D., & Olsen, C. R. An overview. In H. W. Hickey & C. Van Voorhees (Eds.), *The role of the school in community education.* Midland, Mich.: Pendell Publishing, 1969.

Muntyan, M. Community school concepts: A critical analysis. In N. Henry (Ed.), *National Society for the Study of Education: 52nd yearbook, part II, the community school.* Chicago: University of Chicago Press, 1953.

Seay, M. F. The community school emphasis in the post-war period. In N. Henry (Ed.), *National Society for the Study of Education: 44th yearbook, part I, American education in the post-war period.* Chicago: University of Chicago Press, 1945.

Whitt, R. L. *A handbook for the community school director.* Midland, Mich.: Pendell Publishing, 1971.

". . . the differences between community education and community services are that community education is a philosophical concept which, in addition to meeting the educational needs and preferences of community members, utilizes a local agency (usually the public schools) as a catalyst for community development; whereas, community services are action programs of the two-year college through which the College can serve as an agency of community education." — Oravecz

Chapter 4

The Role of the Two Year College in Community Education

by
Michael T. Oravecz

THE ROLE OF THE TWO YEAR COLLEGE IN COMMUNITY EDUCATION

When attempting to define the role of the two-year college in community education, one must remain cognizant of the fact that there are more than 1000 two-year colleges in the United States, each having as its goal the development of an educational program which serves the unique needs of the communities which constitute its service area. Thus, only in a general sense can the role of the community college, or any two-year college, in community education be discussed.

The typical composition of an educational program of a community college has been identified (Heath & Seay, 1974) as containing a transfer function, an occupational career or vocational/technical function, and a community service function. The educational program of a two-year branch campus is typically composed of the transfer and community service functions; while that of a two-year technical college, includes the vocational/technical and community service functions.

The transfer function serves the preparatory needs of students who desire a professional or baccalaureate degree. The vocational/technical function serves the needs of students who desire two-year preparation for entering a vocation. The community service function is a function of the two-year college which accepts its role as one of the educational agencies in a local community. It is solely in regard to the latter function that the role of the two-year college in community education is most often considered. This is a mistake. When discussing the role of the two-year college in community education one must consider all the educational functions performed by the college or else there is an impression that community education is an add on to the regular program.

The mistake is made when the terms community education and community service are used interchangeably. I wish to emphasize that they are not synonymous. While recognizing that attempts to define these terms incur disagreements, I believe that not doing so invites confusion. Furthermore, as the economist Bish (1971) so wisely points out, "continuing academic inquiry faces almost insuperable difficulties when scholars are unable to agree even on common definitions for important words in their working vocabularies" (p. 13). Hence, I propose that we use the following definitions. The first, for community education, is adapted from one suggested by Jack Minzey (1974). The second, for community services, is adapted from a definition offered by Gunder Myran (1971).

Community Education is a philosophical concept which serves the entire community by providing for all the educational needs and preferences of the community members, and by using a local agency as the catalyst for bringing community resources to bear on community problems in an effort to develop a positive sense of community, improve community living and develop a community process toward the end of self-actualization.

Community Services are those action programs of the two-year college, undertaken independently or in cooperation with other community groups and agencies, which direct the unique educational resources of the college toward meeting individual, group, and community educational needs and preferences.

There are important differences in these definitions which require some elaboration. First, community education is a *philosophical concept,* whereas, community services are *action programs.* This is an important distinction. Too often community education is considered programmatically. Community education is not a combination of unrelated programs, nor an addition to an existing educational structure. As a philosophy community education is based on a set of observations:

1) all learning does not take place solely within the traditional educational institutions found in a community — e.g., schools, two-year colleges, proprietary schools, and the like;
2) the need for learning activities transcends the traditional groups for which educational experiences are normally provided — e.g., K-12 students, the 18 to 24 year olds, etc.;
3) learning activities found within a community are generally disjointed, unstructured, and uncoordinated;
4) ignorance and naivete as to what is occurring in the local environment are detriments to the community's development; and
5) people are rational and know what is in their best interests and when provided with sufficient information they will make appropriate decisions.

Thus, community education as a philosophy consists of a concern for the traditional educational programs within a community but advocates: 1) expanding all types of activities for children; 2) making the traditional programs more relevant to the needs of the community; 3) providing equal educational opportunities for adults in all areas of education (recreational, vocational, avocational, and social as well as academic); 4) greater use of all facilities in the community; 5) the identification and coordination of community resources in order to solve community problems; and 6) organizing the community on the local level in order to identify resources, needs and problems, and to work toward the solution of these problems.

A second difference is that community education includes bringing total community resources to bear on community problems — i.e., a community development role. This includes resources other than educational resources meeting needs and preferences other than educational needs and preferences. However, the definition of community services recognizes that a two-year college derives its legitimacy as an institution from its educational role and, therefore, community service activities are legitimate only to the extent that they extend and expand the unique educational resources of the college toward meeting the educational needs and preferences of the community. As Max Raines (1971) has stated:

> If a line needs to be drawn to determine what kinds of activities are to be included in the community services program it must be drawn on the basis of the educational implication of the activity. In short, community colleges are in the business of education and their activities should reflect appropriate relationships to the educational process. (p. 405)

Thirdly, the catalyst for implementing the community education concept must be a local agency, or in the case of an urban area a "neighborhood" agency. Because of the human and physical resources available to it, the local agency is usually the public school. However, like Maurice Seay (1975), I believe that in the absense of the local agency's involvement, or at the urging of community agencies wishing to be involved in community education and seeking leadership, the community college should stimulate and coordinate a community education program but only while offering encouragement and leadership to local agencies in their service area to assume the role as catalyst.

THE COMPONENTS OF THE COMMUNITY EDUCATION PHILOSOPHY

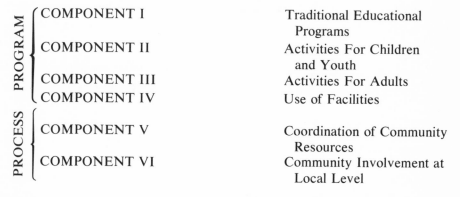

PROGRAM	COMPONENT I	Traditional Educational Programs
	COMPONENT II	Activities For Children and Youth
	COMPONENT III	Activities For Adults
	COMPONENT IV	Use of Facilities
PROCESS	COMPONENT V	Coordination of Community Resources
	COMPONENT VI	Community Involvement at Local Level

Figure 4-1

If one considers that a community college's service area is composed of politically and demographically separate communities or that the amount of local control varies according to state legislative directives and the degree of state centralization, then it's illogical to assume that a two-year college can serve as an effective catalyst at the local level for any length of time. Likewise, it's illogical to assume that a local agency can effectively serve as a catalyst beyond its confines. So, the community college could help fill the gaps from its perspective as an educational agency for the whole community or service area.

In summary, then, the differences between community education and community services are that community education is a philosophical concept which, in addition to meeting the educational needs and preferences of community members, utilizes a local agency (usually the public schools) as a catalyst for community development; whereas, community services are action programs of the two-year college through which the college can serve as an agency for community education.

As previously mentioned, the definitions for community education and community services were adapted from those found in the literature. One noteworthy change is the addition of the word *preferences* to both definitions. Even though the terms needs and preferences are often used interchangeably, they are subtly different. A *need* refers to something essential or desirable that is lacking as measured against an arbitrarily defined standard or norm. A *preference* is a choice given priority over others as determined through a collective decision making process or some other measurement of group or individual choices.

For example, activities designed to ascertain the illiteracy rate in a community would be classified as determining a need since illiteracy is defined in terms of an arbitrary standard; whereas, determining what courses to offer via a survey submitted to the community is measuring preferences.

Having defined terms it is now possible to consider the role of the two-year college in community education. Basically its role can be viewed as activities responding to the educational needs and preferences of the community; activities that are commensurate with the educational process — namely, teaching, research, and evaluation; activities that reflect the educational program of a two-year college and its unique resources; and, very importantly, activities that are developed from careful studies of local factors. These activities can best be described by considering the community service function of the two-year college.

A distinction will be made between those activities that constitute the community services program and those that are process or programming activities. The conceptual framework for making the differences understood is systems theory. In the context of systems theory the two-year college is viewed as one element of a number of elements which interact interdependently. In simplest terms, the college takes resources (its inputs) from a larger system or environment (its service area), processes these resources (I refer to this as programming), and returns them in changed form as output (programs).

Thus, the role of the two-year college in community education will be defined through a model consisting of the systems input-process-output cycle, where the environment phase is related to the community or service area served by the college; the input phase consists of the resources available to the college; the process phase is related to programming (activities for developing and insuring continuation of a role in community education); and the output phase consists of programs (activities commensurate with the community's educational needs and preferences).

Identification of the elements (components) of each phase of the model was made largely from a survey of studies and other publications focusing upon community service programs and administration, and community education. The input phase is based upon a national study of community education goals by Donald Weaver (1972). In that study Weaver identified four inputs — human, economic, structural, and physical. After surveying the literature on community services, I concluded that these same four input components were applicable to this model as well.

The human element of the input phase includes the faculty, staff, and students of the college; administrators and members of the governing board of the college; personnel of the various community groups, agencies, and organizations; and individual members of the community. The economic component consists of the method and amount of financing available for community services and the various socio-economic conditions found within the community. The structural element refers to how community services are organized and staffed; the amount and type of leadership community services receive; and the legal controls placed on the college by legislative fiat. The physical component consists of available college and community building facilities.

The document which contributed most significantly to the remaining phases of this model was Max Raines' (1971) *Taxonomy of Community Services* which was developed through an examination of the variety of community services programs in the United States and reviewed by several authorities in the field of community services. The taxonomy is divided into three major categories, each category containing six separate functions. Careful examination of the descriptions of each of the eighteen functions resulted in my deciding that eight of the functions met my definition of programming and ten functions my definition of program.

Support for using the eighteen functions as elements in the model came from studies by Harlacher (1969) and others, plus the fact that the twenty-three services listed in the program guide of the National Council on Community Services can be correlated with the functions selected as program components. It should also be noted that the model is consistent with the taxonomy of community services developed from a 1974 study conducted by the Florida Community/Junior College Interinstitutional Research Council (Nickens, 1976) which have been incorporated in the model.

Those functions meeting the definition of programming are:

- *Advisory Liason:* identifying and involving (in an advisory capacity) key members of the various subgroups with whom cooperative efforts are being planned — e.g., community services advisory council, *ad hoc* advisory committees, etc.
- *Community Analysis:* collecting and analyzing data which reflect existing and emerging needs and preferences of the community and which serve as a basis for developing the college's role in community education — e.g., analyzing census tracts, analyzing man-power data, conducting problem-oriented studies, identifying roles and goals of organization, etc.
- *Public Information:* interpreting programs and activities of community services to the college staff as well as to the community at large and coordinating releases with the central information services of the college.
- *Program Management:* establishing procedures for procuring and allocating the physical and human resources necessary to implement the community services program — e.g., staff recruitment, job descriptions, budgetary development, etc.
- *Program Evaluation:* developing with the staff the specific objectives of the program, identifying sources of data, and establishing procedures for gathering data to appraise the probable effectiveness of various facets of the program — e.g., participant ratings, attendance patterns, behavioral changes, program requests, etc.
- *Staff Development:* providing opportunities and encouragement for staff members to up-grade their skills in program development and evaluation — e.g., professional affiliations, exchange visitations, professional conferences, advanced graduate studies, etc.
- *Facility Utilization:* encouraging community use of college facilities by making them readily accessible, by facilitating the scheduling process, and by designing them for multipurpose activities when appropriate — e.g., plan campus tours, create a centralized scheduling office, conference rooms, auditorium design, etc.
- *Interagency Cooperation:* establishing adequate linkage with related

programs of the college and the community to supplement and coordinate rather than unnecessarily duplicate existing programs — e.g., calendar coordination, information exchange, joint committee work, etc.

A ninth function, not previously defined anywhere, but very important is,

- *Intracollege Cooperation:* establishing adequate linkage with departments within the college to supplement and coordinate rather than duplicate programs and to identify and develop the college's unique resources — e.g., coordinating committees, contact persons, information exchange, joint committee work, etc.

The functions which comprise the program (output) phase of the model are:

- *Personal Counseling:* opportunities for community members for self-discovery and development through individual and group counseling processes — e.g., aptitude-interest testing, individual interviews, career information, job placement, family life, etc.
- *Educational Extension:* increasing the accessibility of the courses and curricula of the college by extending their availability to the community-at-large — e.g., evening classes, TV courses, offering courses on weekends, neighborhood extension centers, etc.
- *Educational Expansion:* educational upgrading and new career opportunities which reach beyond the traditional limitations of college credit restrictions — e.g., workshops, seminars, tours, short courses, in-plant training, etc.
- *Constituency Development:* programs to increase the earning power, educational level, and political influence of disadvantaged — e.g., ADC mothers, unemployed, educationally deprived youth, underemployed welfare recipients, etc.
- *Cultural Development:* opportunities for community members to participate in a variety of cultural activities — e.g., fine art series, art festivals, artists in residence, community theater, etc.
- *Leisure-Time Activity:* opportunities for community members to participate in a variety of recreational activities — e.g., sports instruction, outdoor education, summer youth programs, senior citizen activities, etc.
- *Public Forum:* activities designed to stimulate interest and understanding of local, national, and world problems — e.g., public affairs pamphlets, "town" meetings, TV symposiums, radio programs, etc.
- *Civic Action:* participating in cooperative efforts with local government, business, industry, professions, religious and social groups to increase the resources of the community to deal with major problems

confronting the community — e.g., community self-studies, urban beautification, United Torch drives, air pollution, etc.

- *Staff Consultation:* making available the consulting skills of the faculty in community development activities — e.g., consulting with small businesses, advising on instructional techniques, designing community studies, instructing in group leadership, laboratory testing etc.
- *Conference Planning:* providing professional assistance to community groups in the planning of conferences, institutes, and workshops — e.g., registration procedures, program development, conference evaluation, etc.

and an eleventh component, defined because nothing was found in Raines' taxonomy to correspond to a category in Harlacher's study, is

- *Agency Organization:* assisting in the establishment, coordination, and sustenance of needed community groups — e.g., mutual arts association, area arts councils, council of social agencies, area audio-visual materials center, etc.

A comprehensive view of the model is found below.

I suggest that colleges select from this model those activities which they deem appropriate to their role in community education. The extent to which any are judged appropriate should be determined by the college's educational mission, the unique resources of the college, and the community's educational needs and preferences.

Figure 4-2

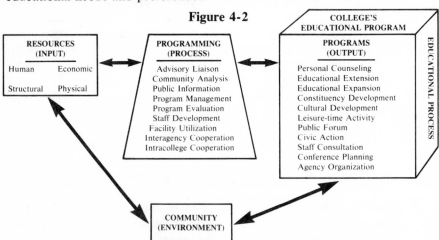

COMMUNITY SERVICES: A SYSTEMS MODEL APPROACH

REFERENCES

Bish, R. L. *The public economy of metropolitan areas.* Chicago: Rand McNally College Publishing, 1971.

Harlacher, E. L. *The community dimension of the community college.* Englewood Cliffs, New Jersey: Prentice-Hall, 1969.

Heath, P. R., & Seay, M. F. The role of the community college in community education. In M. F. Seay & Associates, *Community education: A developing concept.* Midland, Michigan: Pendell Publishing, 1974.

Minzey, J. D. It takes people to make it happen. *Community Education Journal*, 1974, *4* (1), 46-50.

Myran, G. A. *Community services perceptions of the national council on community services.* East Lansing, Michigan: Kellogg Community Services Leadership Program, Michigan State University, 1971.

Nickens, J. M. A taxonomy for community services. *New Directions For Community Colleges,* Summer 1976, (14), 11-18.

Raines, M. R. A taxonomy of community services. In W. K. Ogilive & M. R. Raines (Eds.) *Perspectives on the community-junior college.* New York: Appleton-Century-Crofts, 1971.

Seay, M. F. The role of the community college in community education. *Community Education Journal,* 1975, *5* (1), 33-34.

Weaver, D. C. *The emerging community education model.* Kalamazoo, Michigan: Mott Leadership Program, Western Michigan University, 1972.

"Whereas there is much that is educationally and socially attractive about community development and community education, there is also a critical, initial *need to place the tangible program ideas and organizational possibilities in some substantial philosophical context."* — Fitzgerald

Chapter 5

Community Education — A Cause Without Reason

by

Barry C. Fitzgerald

COMMUNITY EDUCATION: A CAUSE WITHOUT A REASON?

Community Education is a term that holds various connotations for educational leaders in Australia. Some are doubtless curious about this much discussed recent development; some are probably already committed to establishing a closer form of relationship between their schools and the community in which they stand; some are possibly openly cynical, hostile, or quietly apathetic about this new piece of educational ballyhoo and who will want to stand recorded on the "I told you so" roll of honour. Many will be seeking new ideas in the interpersonal and inter-group communication that usually stems from a study of community education.

As educational leaders we are failing in our prime role of leadership if we approach this important educational concept in the same way we might approach a visit to the Royal Show or a Homes Exhibition — gathering in haphazard fashion, lots of colorful and attractive tidbits and odds and ends that, when they are later examined, turn out to be cheap, shoddy, or irrelevant to our needs. Many conferences on community education, for example, are characterized by participants collecting brochures, simulation games, program details, and the like. Folder-filling mania appears to be a major activity.

Whereas there is much that is educationally and socially attractive about community development and community education, there is also a critical, *initial* need to place the tangible program ideas and organizational possibilities in some substantial philosophical context. How we approach this task will, of course, depend on our individual personalities, social attitudes, educational philosophies, and upon the particular social context in which our professional role is played out. But, this task *must* be tackled if we are to avoid a charge of gathering pretty baubles in the instinctive way of the magpie or bower bird.

THE USA LESSON

In facing this challenge, Australian educators can learn much, good and bad, from the current American educational scene. For example, a look at projects in places like Flint (Michigan), Minneapolis (Minnesota), Atlanta (Georgia), and elsewhere reveals a great deal about the various forms of municipal-school agreements, of joint funding arrangements, of university training programs, of building use and design, of program possibilities, and the like.

However, one aspect of the development of community education in the USA that can be criticized is the absence of any continuing, serious attempt to establish a social or educational theory to support the concept. While the popular texts in the area (Minzey & LeTarte, 1972; Seay, 1974; and the like) do contain elements of theoretical discussion, they do not provide substantial theoretical analysis or debate.

Many papers that evince an interest in analysing the rationale for community education have failed to grapple seriously with the problem. For example, a paper by Douglas (1971) titled *The Community School Philosophy and the Inner City School* makes predictable observations such as "education is a total community concern enlisting the services of all citizens as they are needed and can contribute" (p. 331), and "the community schools serve all of the community's inhabitants" (p. 331). What is surprising, however, is the simplistic conclusion that such platitudinous comment constitutes an attempt "to define the community school concept or philosophy" (p. 332.)

Similarly, an examination of the various programs at national or international conferences on community education also indicates an almost total lack of concern with the development of an adequate theoretical base. Rather, conferences have become anecdotal in nature, reviewing programs and innovatory ideas and comparing notes on funding and legislative developments. For example, the emphasis of a three-day conference on community education in Las Vegas in May, 1976, was upon the need for increased funding from the Mott Foundation. This disproportionate concern with programs and funding has resulted in a serious weakness in research and philosophical debate.

One reason for this situation has been the *human* factor. Until recently, the majority of community educators in the USA have been personable and practical people with substantial responsibilities for program development, consultation, preparation of submissions and proposals, various forms of public relations exercises, and building supervision. The nature of their work responsibilities, their professional experience, their academic studies, and the personal interests of many community education personnel have been contributory factors in the preeminent focus on the tangible aspects of program development and people involvement.

Another factor which has diverted attention from theory development has been the continuing need to justify the community education concept in terms of annual counts of classes, programs, and people. State funding provisions rely predominantly on a dubious head-counting exercise; local school boards and voters, not unnaturally, have equated numbers with educational and social effectiveness. Such demands are frequent and time-consuming.

To date, for reasons such as these, the concern has been with the *who* (the clients, the directors, the teachers), with the *what* (the programs and proposals), with the *how* (the techniques of administration and coordination), with virtually no attention being paid to the *why* of community development in schools and education. Themes and concerns of books, films, papers, and conferences in this area further emphasize this point. As a consequence, there have been some substantial-looking castles built of shiny, colorful baubles.

The reason for bemoaning this pattern of development in the United States has been to sound a warning that a similar pattern is developing in this country. Of course, once more, it's perfectly understandable in the first few years of attempting to establish a credibility and viability for the concept of community education, that great emphasis should be placed on getting the score on the board, getting programs moving, getting needs catered for.

But in the face of educational, academic, and public questioning of and interest in this concept: Is it worthwhile having a cause without reason?

A SCOTTISH LEAD

As a starting point in identifying some theoretical bases for the community education concept, it is useful to look at the development of the school-community relationship in another country — Scotland.

In 1970, a select committee, chaired by K. J. W. Alexander, Professor of Economics at Strathclyde University, was formed to:

> . . . consider the aims appropriate to voluntary leisure time courses for adults which are educational but not specifically vocational; to examine the extent to which these are being achieved at present; and, with due regard to the need to use available resources most effectively, to make recommendations. (Alexander, 1975, p. vi)

The findings of this committee were published in 1975 in a report titled *Adult Education: The Challenge of Change*. Included in the 66 recommendations was the major one that "the Secretary of State should establish a Scottish Council for Community Education" (pp. 57-58).

But it is not so much the political, structural, and procedural suggestions that are of importance in today's context. Rather, it is the analysis by the committee of the *reasons* for the various specific recommendations. While recognizing the inherent power of education as an agent of social change, the committee attempted to provide an analysis of the forces, especially those of technology, economics, politics, and social structures, that were changing the shape and responsibilities of the educational system.

Let's consider some of these and consider their implications for education and its growing concern with community.

The Alexander Report identified five main areas of change: technological, demographic, political, psychological, and educational system. While some of the examples of social change are obvious ones, and have been pointed to on many occasions by sociologists and by "popular" writers such as McLuhan, Packard, and Toffler, their relevance to the community education debate had been considered indirectly at best prior to the Alexander Report.

A review of the kinds of social changes referred to in the Alexander Report and in other contemporary analyses may provide a useful basis from which to attempt to develop a rationale for the community education concept. The lists which follow are suggestive rather than complete.

Technological Changes. Many recent technological developments appear to have implications for education. For example:

1. There are new productive processes requiring a new match of human and technical skills.
2. There are the new products which have arisen from advanced technology and which require new skills for their use (calculators, computers, copiers, etc.).
3. There are changed job circumstances as a result of new technologies. Emery (1974), for example, claimed that in every technology "we are finding that instrumentation, automation and computerization are transforming the interface between man and machine or plant" (p. 67).
4. There have been advances in medicine and pharmacology, especially as they relate to the very young and very old.
5. There is the matter of the environmental impact of technical advances (home accidents, pesticides, etc.).
6. There are changes in occupational mobility and in consequent social mobility; Emery (1974) suggested that "the concept of a lifetime career is unlikely to survive past 1980 . . . The expectation will be that a person will branch out in different directions at different stages of his life" (p. 66).
7. There is development in scope and influence of entertainment and the media (radio, TV, paperback revolution).

The Alexander report seemed to be asking the question: "Who has the educational responsibilities inherent in such changing technological circumstances?"

Demographic Changes. Likewise, there are generalizations that could be made in this area:

1. There are changing patterns in employment resulting in a "blurring or changing in long established distinctions of status, and introducing new hierarchies within occupations, industry and society" (Alexander Report, p. 22).
2. There is the phenomenon of increased residential mobility.
3. There are the changing proportions of the young and old in the population.
4. There is the growth in leisure time and the associated implications for life style, economics, education, and politics. Emery (1974) claimed that the growth in leisure and leisure-related durables and services will create new patterns of living (such as a pattern of *saving to spend* rather than *saving for a rainy day*).

In this respect, it is interesting to note the findings of a recent *Age* poll (March 30, 1977) which reported that 66 percent of respondents considered that "now is a good time to spend" (p. 5). The poll data are shown in Figure 5-1.

But while there is a widespread acceptance that industrial societies are entering a leisure age, Caldwell (1976) cited Australian data which suggested that the emergence of substantially greater periods of leisure for the workforce is not as dramatic as has been believed. He reported that, in Australia, in the 1969 to 1974 period, "the average weekly working hours for males has hovered around the 41 hour mark — 40.8 (1969), 41.2 (1970), 41.1 (1971), 40.7 (1972), 41.9 (1973), and 41.6 (1974)" (p. 7).

What appears to be happening in countries like Britain and the USA is that leisure time is used for overtime or a second job, which may account for the relatively stable worksheet statistics. Again, such a phenomenon has obvious social and educational implications.

Psychological Changes. In this area, a brief statement from Alvin Toffler's (1974) book, *Learning for Tomorrow,* provides an excellent summary of the kinds of points raised in the Alexander Report. Toffler wrote:

> In industry, for example, workers are rated, selected and placed in different jobs; job success is predicted; work environments are studied and manipulated with an eye to changing future productivity levels, job satisfaction, or accident rates; man-machine relationships are investigated to increase efficiency or to reduce fatigue; work groups and organizations are studied in order to improve communications or to reduce intergroup tensions; and individuals are studied to learn how to increase motivation and morale and to reduce boredom and monotony. (p. 95)

ATTITUDES TO SPENDING OR SAVING - 1

(Rated by Sex, Occupation, Voting Intention, and State)

	Total	Male	Female	Blue Collar Workers	White Collar Workers	Will Vote ALP.	Will vote LIB.	NSW.	VIC.	Qld.
	(1,980)	(965)	(1,015)	(1,015)	(844)	(859)	(771)	(769)	(625)	(297)
A	66%	68%	64%	60%	72%	59%	73%	64%	67%	61%
B	30	27	32	36	22	36	22	32	28	32
C	5	5	5	4	6	5	5	4	5	6

A = It is sensible to buy things now because they may be more expensive later.

B = It is not wise to spend money now because the future is too uncertain.

C = Don't know.

AUSTRALIA

Figure 5-1.

"Attitudes to Spending or Saving, Australia 1977," *The Age*, March 30, 1977, p. 5.

Once more the question remains: Where do education and the schools come into this?

Political Change. While many school curricular statements continue to espouse goals of preparing students to become "good citizens" or to "take their place in a democratic way of life," the realities of recent political developments in many western countries suggest that a substantial basis of political change has occurred.

1. There has been a growth in public disillusionment with politics and with the political community. These attitudes were dramatically evident in the post-Watergate period in the United States. Similar attitudes have been seen in the results of the public opinion polls conducted in Australia, even prior to the Watergate hearings. Nisbet (1973) said that "the waning of the political community in the West is one of the most fateful changes now to be seen . . . Trust, confidence and belief in the political state is at an all time low in the United States and other countries as well. Equally serious is the low ebb of interest in or motivation toward, politics and political authority" (p. 17).

2. There has been the emergence of the concept of shared resources and financial responsibility between various facets of government, federal, state and local, and between public and private groups or agencies.

3. There has been the emergence of new groups which are politically informed and concerned with the acquisition of power (tenants' unions, migrant groups, women's groups, and the like). Bases of power and processes of decision-making are under more frequent and direct scrutiny. Even teachers have entered the exercise of power acquisition. Johnston (1974), for example, claimed:

   > A prominent feature of many contemporary, industrialized societies has been the rising demand by various occupational associations, from those for unskilled to those for professional workers, for a greater degree of self-determination. One manifestation of this trend has been the pressure by teachers for an enlarged role in the control of the education budget. Teacher organizations in the United States, England, and Australia have demonstrated through the late sixties and early seventies a growing militancy which has been expressed most consistently in connection with demands for increased power in salary determination. (pp. 113-114)

4. There has been a replacement of some older forms of political and social communities with other forms. Nisbet (1973) pointed to the

evangelical movements and "novel" religions that seemed to hold fascination for widening sectors of the young. He pointed to the relatively recent upthrust of *ethnicity,* with Jews, black, Polish, and Chicanos acquiring new forms of ethnic pride.

In Nisbet's view, the ethnic bond, which is "grounded in history, is proving to be stronger than the often artificial Political bond" (p. 18). He cited the revival of the commune as a social phenomenon of recent years. Local parallels for these changes can readily be found on the Australian scene.

Educational Change. The Alexander Report also reminded that there were changes in education itself that concern this analysis of community and education.

1. There has been the erosion of the assumption that education is a once and for all experience, sufficient to equip people with all the knowledge, techniques, and skills needed for a full life.
2. There has been the acceptance of the proposition that education can no longer be seen as being principally concerned with the development of the intellect. In schools today, pupils are encouraged to participate in a widening range of activities — cultural, social, practical, and recreational, as well as intellectual.
3. There has been the transfer in emphasis from teaching to learning especially individualized learning facilitated by educational technology. The Alexander Report argued that "the significance of this trend is that education need no longer be treated as co-terminous with school, college or university" (p. 24).
4. Consequently, there has been "a widening gap between the experience and understanding of parents regarding the nature and purpose of education and the experience of children" (Alexander, 1975, p. 24).
5. There has been a reassessment of the attitude, especially evident amongst teachers in the sixties, that the involvement of the school with community life and problems would, as a consequence, divert resources and energy from basic academic concerns.

> As Midwinter (1973) put it:
> There were worries that a commitment of school to the social idyll of a regenerated community might lessen the already woebegone performance of socially disadvantaged children in the traditional education stakes. (p. 11)

However, Midwinter claimed:
> Individual treatment is futile if meted out in a social vacuum. It is imperative to ensure that the school and its community coexist in a cosier and less antagonistic fashion. The community school should

provide a wholesome context for that triple partnership of child, parent and teacher which could assume the more fruitful realization of the child's potential. (p. 11)

Furthermore, assurances from formal groups such as the Curriculum Standing Committee for Technical Schools (Victoria, Australia) have allayed some of the "diversion of resources" fear associated with community schools and community education. The Standing Committee stressed that "the major elements of the existing curriculum — e.g., development of literacy and numeracy — would be of corresponding importance in the community school" (Curriculum Standing Committee for Technical Schools, 1971, p. 3).

Change and the New Community. There is, of course, a substantial leap of faith required to accept any proposition that such changes represent any rationale for the introduction of community education in this country. An analysis of the implications of such changes, however, constitutes a necessary step in formulating an adequate theoretical statement. Let us accept the general social, political, technological, and educational picture that has been presented as being essentially accurate. The constant dynamic present in all levels and in all examples is that of change: change in work; change in leisure; change in personal relationships; change in life-style; change in political expectations; change in environmental, moral, and social values — the list goes on.

Long ago, commentators such as Ferdinand Tonnies (1887) anticipated the effects of such change on social life and organization. Social anonymity, the increase in the control of law, occupational specialization, personal and social mobility were all seen as consequences of twentieth-century living.

But while this pattern of change has brought with it the demise of some forms of traditional community groupings, the basic human need for interaction and affection has resulted in the emergence of newer or perhaps more recently apparent forms of community. As referred to earlier, Nisbet (1973) pointed to several forms. Take religion. He claimed that while "the authority of the great organized religions seems to be at a very low point today . . . there is the unmistakable growth of membership in some of the most fundamentalist of religions" (p. 17). He pointed to examples such as the evangelical movement and some of the bizarre and novel hybrid religions formed from Eastern and Western traditions that have so attracted many young people.

It is the younger elements of society that have drawn attention to newer forms rather than to the demise of community. Nisbet argued that "the strength of kinship as a norm today amongst the liberated is in marked contrast to the hostility or contempt in which this norm was held two or three generations ago" (p. 20). The revival of the commune in recent years represents an organizational example of this kinship urge in the young.

This interest in kinship has been paralleled by the emergence of "a new appreciation of co-operation" (Caldwell, 1976, p. 4). Caldwell cited writers who provided explanations of why the younger generation had "turned sour on competition" (p. 4). He appeared to agree with the supporters of social co-operation who argued "that individuals grow by co-operating with one another, trying to contribute to others rather than competing — that greater personal meaningfulness emerges from co-operative interaction as opposed to competitive interfacing" (p. 4).

Perhaps partly reflecting this interest of the young, there has been a general interest in community development in most age groups in recent years. For example, the Australian Assistance Plan (1975), "a national experimental program to get people together to improve their own community in the way they want" (p. 3), was implemented in 1975. The basic concept underlying this plan was a concern with development of community and social planning. Midwinter (1973) had suggested that such community development relies on two features. The first is the provision of resources to needy areas "to meet the intertwined problems of welfare, education, transport, housing, employment, personal services and public activities" (p. 12).

But it is Midwinter's second feature that may provide a substantial component of the argument for community education. This feature of community development requires the introduction of "some form of interdisciplinary administration based securely on the popular participation of the residents and others in the community" (p. 12). Such participation, Midwinter suggested, would fail if the participants had not been educated for their role. Indeed:

> It is the necessary task of the Community School to service the community with socially articulate citizens who, initially, can organize themselves competently enough to press for an improved environment and afterwards to manage it efficiently. (p. 13)

A Social Imbalance. The present concern with community — whatever it means — has possibly come about for one basic reason. In contemporary times there has developed a critical social imbalance between the kind of human needs that concern people, and the ability of the social structure to provide for these needs.

Furthermore, education, in general, has a substantial role to play in redressing this imbalance. Perhaps the nature of this imbalance can be illustrated by referring to earlier forms of social organization.

Under the social conditions of older societies, the importance of the satisfaction of needs such as food and individual and group safety were reflected in residential patterns, in personal relationships, and in social habits. For example, towns and villages were walled, people lived close to the sources of food, there was considerable interdependence in work and production, interpersonal contacts were extensive, family ties were close. There was a balance between social need and social structure and characteristics.

Trethwey (1974), one of the few writers to have shown a concern for development of a rationale for the new school-community relationship, suggested that a rationale which is dependent upon the "loss of community" hypothesis is usually based upon some variation of this rural model of community.

Such communities, usually rural, were perceived to be characterised by (i) a small population, (ii) stability of population, (iii) employment within the area of residence, (iv) employment within a limited range of occupations known and understood by most people, (v) frequent contact in work and social activities by people within the locality, (vi) an extended family pattern, (vii) interdependent relationships between people, (and) (viii) convergent values. (Trethewey, 1974, p. 44)

But today, people appear to be threatened and not facilitated by prevalent social factors such as the increasing isolation of the individual, the specialization and turnover of labour, and the growing influence of law and social restriction in the life of modern man. Increasingly, factors such as population mobility are seen to be having an important influence on the lives of people and of communities. The Royal Automobile Club, Victoria (RACV), for example, has noted that an average of 7,500 of their approximately 650,000 members change their address each month (Daffey, 1977).

In this kind of social, context, Trethewey (1974) argued: . . . there is a more tenuous, unstable and spatially extensive network of social interaction producing less sense of place and belonging, less participation and security and even a sense of isolation, anonymity, lack of identity, lack of involvement, even alienation, that is, loss of community. (p. 45)

Trethewey's generalizations accord closely with the position taken by the English community educationist, Poster (1971), who characterized the basic problem of modern society as "rootless" and "meaningless" lives being experienced by people. Poster was "disturbed by disorganisation, dislocation and what he sees as a breakdown in social order" (Thorpe, 1973, p. 38).

It's in this kind of *anomie* interpretation of contemporary society, perhaps linked with the alienation theories preferred by writers such as

Midwinter (1972) and Jackson (1973), that a satisfactory explanation can be found for the current interest in the school and community relationship. Thorpe (1973), too, suggested that "it is perhaps the dual themes of anomie and alienation which provide the reasons why the community school is currently fashionable on the educational scene" (p. 38).

Such theoretical themes appear to be reflected in the emergence of groups such as citizens' advice bureaux, learning exchanges, free legal services, lifeline, community development groups, joint municipal-school ventures, and the like. Developments such as these reflect some of the social features peculiar to recent times: people are seeking advice and direction, people are confused by bureaucracies, people are searching for identity and self-fulfillment, people are looking for ways to use the time that lays heavily on their hands. In short, people have social and personal needs that are not being met by traditional structures or agencies.

While some of us may perhaps be inclined to dismiss the development of these groups as passing fads, it is more probable that there will be a *proliferation* rather than a disappearance of such groups and organizations in the years ahead.

This belief is supported by an analysis of the nature of contemporary human needs. Maslow (1954), for example, contended that man has five basic needs, and that human behaviour can largely be explained by man's attempt to satisfy them. The categories of these hierarchical needs are those of food, safety, love and affection, the desire for esteem of others, and the need for a sense of adequacy or self-fulfillment. For most people in the Australian society of today, the food and safety needs have been met, and, as a consequence, the needs for acceptance, esteem, and self-fulfillment have become important. But rather than reflecting present-day human needs, the characteristics of contemporary Western society are such that needs are intensified rather than satisfied.

If Maslow is to be believed, we need love and affection from others, yet we live in a society characterized by social anonymity; we need to have a sense of esteem, yet we live in a society which is in a state of geographical flux, where people are likely to move before they come to know one another; we have more time to create or express or develop new and satisfying skills, yet, until recently, most community resources were closed or not easily accessible to us.

The kinds of agencies and groups mentioned previously reflect a grass roots attempt to provide for such expressed community needs. People from the learning-centre type of organization, for example, could give detailed testimony to the ways in which such needs have affected the lives of many people lost in suburbia. Wesson (1975) has gathered many statements of this need in her book. There is little doubt that we have available the physical and human resources appropriate for coping with the changes mentioned herein and for catering for the kinds of human need listed by Maslow and articulated by Wesson's contributors. What has been lacking is the co-ordination and application of social resources to the situation we would all have recognized. Take recreation as just one example. For several decades in this country, people have had the need of self-developing and fulfilling recreational, leisure, or simple togetherness activities; yet it has only been in very recent years that federal, state, and local governments have moved to provide meaningful leadership, funding, and facilities.

Which brings us back to the community and education relationship. Obviously schools, teachers, and other facets of education represent a substantial human and physical resource and must join with other public resources in reviewing their function and potential. In recent years parents have come to recognize this and have come to demand their piece of the action. The community involvement in school-decision-making issue has, in the past twelve months, become the most discussed and debated issue in Australian education, and this phenomenon is part of a general political concern permeating our school system.

SUMMARY

What, then, is the *why* of all this? *Why* are schools becoming more community oriented? *Why* has the community education concept gained such sudden visibility in this country? *Why* should schools suddenly find themselves sharing the educational scene with informal learning groups? *Why* should the Australian College of Education focus its 1977 Conference on this education area? No answers to all of these questions have been posited. However, our thinking on such questions should be supported by some satisfactory educational or social rationale. Some possible components of such a rationale have been offered. Until such components are more satisfactorily integrated into a coherent theory the community education concept cannot claim the serious attention of educators or public. The case that community education is important because it encourages multi-use of facilities and results in various economic advantages must rest upon more basic social, political, or educational theory. Serious and protracted debate of principles and rationale must precede or at least run parallel to the identification and solution of the practical problems associated with this concept. Unless this happens, community education in Australia and elsewhere will probably remain a cause without reason.

REFERENCES

Alexander, K. J. W. (Chair). *Adult education: The challenge of change* (Report by Committee of Inquiry appointed by Secretary of State for Scotland). Edinburgh: HMSO, 1975.

Attitudes to spending or saving, Australia 1977. *The Age,* March 30, 1977, p. 5.

Caldwell, G. *Some developments in education, work and leisure and the future of the work and leisure ethics.* Paper presented at the 47th Congress of the Australian and New Zealand Association for the Advancement of Science, Canberra, May 10-14, 1976.

Curriculum Standing Committee for Technical Schools. *The community school. Melbourne: Education Department (Victoria), 1971. (Document No. AC71/510)*

Department of Social Security. *People power: Australian assistance plan.* Canberra: Australian Government Publishing Service, 1975.

Douglas, L. The community school philosophy and the inner-city school. *Urban Education,* 1971, 5, 328-335.

Emery, F., & Others. *Futures we're in.* Canberra: Australian National University, Centre for Continuing Education, 1974.

Jackson, B. *How the poorest live: Education. New Society,* February 1973, pp. 229-231.

Johnston, G. L. Who should control the schools? *Journal of Educational Administration,* 1974, *12,* 112-122.

Midwinter, E. The EPA community school. *Urban Education,* 1973, *8,* 7-19.

Midwinter, E. *Projections: An educational priority area at work.* London: Ward Lock, 1972.

Minzey, J., & LeTarte, C. *Community education: From program to process.* Midland, Mich.: Pendell Publishing Co., 1972.

Nisbet, R. The quest for community. *Dialogue,* 1973, *6,* 13-21.

Poster, C. *The school and the community.* London: Macmillan, 1971.

Seay, M. (Ed.). *Community education: A developing concept.* Midland, Mich.: Pendell Publishing Co., 1974.

Thorpe, E. Community schools: Towards a definition. *Education in the North,* 1973, *10,* 33-39.

Toffler, A. *Learning for tomorrow.* New York: Vintage Books, 1974.

Tonnies, F. *(Community and society)* (C. P. Loomis, Ed. and trans.). East Lansing: Michigan State University Press, 1957. (Originally published, 1887.)

Trethewey, A. Rationales offered for new community-school relations in England, the United States of America and Australia. In R. T. Fitzgerald (Ed.), *Community participation and school policy*. Hawthorn: Australian Comparative Education Society, 1974.

Wesson, G. (Ed.). *Brian's wife: Jenny's mum*. Caulfield: Dove Communication, 1975.

PART II

THE COMMUNITY EDUCATOR

"No group can claim professional standing without demonstrable statements as to what constitutes minimal competence in their respective fields. Additionally, sources and level of attainment, as well as means of assessment, are required." — *Miller and McCleary*

Chapter 6

Competency-Based Training Programs In Community Education

by
Brian P. Miller
and
Lloyd E. McCleary

COMPETENCY-BASED TRAINING PROGRAMS IN COMMUNITY EDUCATION

INTRODUCTION

In the development of community education as a profession, it has become increasingly evident that there is a need to define competencies. No group can claim professional standing without demonstrable statements as to what constitutes minimal competence in their respective fields. Additionally, sources and levels of attainment, as well as means of assessment, are required.

With the advent of increased community education programs and the involvement of state and federal agencies, the need for identification of viable community education preservice requirements, state agency requirements, and local educational agency personnel evaluation criteria has increased. Substantive and on-going research and development work in assessing and defining needed competencies in community education is required.

DEFINITION OF COMPETENCY

Before examining competency-based community education administration, it would be well to define the meaning of the term "competency." McCleary and Brown (1973) define competency as "the presence of characteristics or the absence of disabilities which render a person fit, or qualified, to perform a specified task or to assume a defined role." This definition emphasizes two concepts: (1) the specification of defined tasks; and (2) the indication of knowledge or skill needed to perform the tasks.

Perhaps the most applicable model for the development of an integrated and quality development program in community education is that developed by McCleary and Brown (1973). (See Figure 6-1.)

MCCLEARY AND BROWN COMPETENCY MODEL

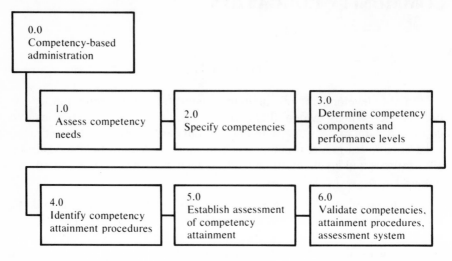

Figure 6-1

ANALYSIS OF COMPETENCY MODEL COMPONENTS

1.0 Assess competency needs

Various methodologies are appropriate in this phase of development. The most efficient and perhaps the most effective, however, is the small group consensus approach. A relatively small group of experienced administrators can provide information about job demands that is sufficiently reliable and accurate. Cross validation can occur later after base line data are gathered about task areas and related competencies.

2.0 Specify competencies

Perhaps the most difficult activity, but a very necessary one, is the actual writing of competency statements. The scope of the statement, its form, and the elements to be included can all create problems. If possible, accept the idea that education (competency attainment) is an open system. This means that all possible competencies will never be identified while some can only be vaguely defined, that some competencies which are identified will not have any identifiable means of attainment, and that some competencies will seem extremely simple and mundane while others will appear to be unrealistic and complex.

Best progress has been made when statements represent an identifiable competency that involves technical, conceptual, and human skills. Some illustrative statements are provided. For the principal a competency statement might be:

The principal needs to know about and be able to employ procedures for establishing organizational goals, clarifying roles, planning, and otherwise providing structure in order for individuals to relate to each other in cooperative and supportive ways.

Where possible the statement should point to a performance expectation that need not be detailed at this point. In the illustration above the statement contains such an expectation: " . . . in order for individuals to relate to each other in cooperative and supportive ways."

Once a set of competency statements have been listed by job category, they should be given priority listing on one or more criteria. Such criteria might be: (1) the importance to success on the job; (2) the extent to which the training program succeeds in developing them to an acceptable level; (3) those competencies which should be given primary attention in pre-service; and (4) those competencies which are best learned on the job.

3.0 Determine competency components and performance levels

A model can best be used to illustrate competency components and performance levels. The model is actually a six-faced cube with six dimensions specified. This display shows only three of the six dimensions. (See Figure 6-2.) A competency statement in the form here advocated is written so that the technical, conceptual, and human components as well as the level of competence (familiarity, understanding, application) can be specified. An illustration of the use of the model to specify components and performance levels is outlined.

Competency statement: "The supervisor will help teachers prepare and use lesson plans."

Familiarity

Technical: The supervisor will examine and record at least three forms of lesson plans and accurately describe them.

Conceptual: The supervisor will explain the uses, compare elements, and identify conditions for use of three forms of lesson plans.

Human: The supervisor will list (in discussion) kinds of problems he might encounter in working with teachers who are not in the habit of using formal lesson plans and indicate suggestions for handling such problems.

Understanding

Technical: The supervisor can take an element of content, specify a learner or learning group, prepare a lesson plan, and "talk through" the lesson or teach it.

Conceptual: The supervisor can analyze the elements in each form of lesson plan and critique them demonstrating that he can recombine elements into a new form, adapt one or more forms to particular uses, etc.

Human: The supervisor will examine situations that illustrate how he or she would work with teachers to teach them lesson planning and to work with them cooperatively in preparing lesson plans (role playing, discussions with supervisors after observation, etc.).

Application

Technical: The supervisor in training will work with supervisors on the job aiding teachers in preparation of lesson plans — writing sample plans, examining and critiquing plans written by others, etc.

Conceptual: The supervisor in training will submit sample plans for criticism by teachers and/or supervisors on the job; he or she will present and explain an analysis of lesson plans prepared by others.

4.0 Identify competency attainment

One means of better allocation of competency attainment is to classify the primary means by which competency is to be attained in a unified program that extends from formal university instruction into on-the-job education in the field. One set of rubrics being tried is to assign primary responsibility for some competency development to formal course work, some to reality oriented experiences, some to integrative experiences, and some to culminating experiences.

COMPETENCY COMPONENT AND PERFORMANCE LEVEL MODEL

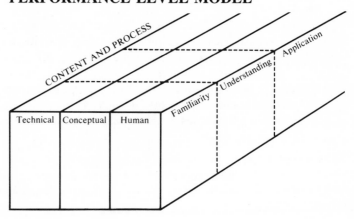

Figure 6-2

Formal courses would provide the knowledge base and be carried on in professor-directed large group settings. Reality oriented experiences would include internships and field experiences under the direct supervision of experiences administrators. Integrative experiences would include seminar or small group sharing, some student directed, in which experiences would be assessed, ideas generated, problems clarified, and solutions explored and related fields examined. Finally, culminating experiences would be largely individual development of performance products that would demonstrate competency attainment, such as designing a new instructional program, planning and conducting an in-service training program, codifying all district policies and preparing a policy book, or serving as chief negotiator in an employee dispute.

5.0 Establish assessment of competency attainment

The identification of instruments and the validation of competence is largely dependent upon the competencies specified and the assignment of competency attainment in the total program of administrative development. The need for precision in defining competencies is brought about by the desire for evaluation. The basis of assessment of the individual's competency attainment is his or her performance. This typically occurs in three areas: (1) products that illustrate capability to perform a function or skill; (2) products that illustrate problem solving capability; and (3) behavior that displays appropriate concern for values exemplified by education. No competency statement should be carried to specification of technical, conceptual, and human component stages without performance specification, and no program should be planned without a clearly designed procedure for competency assessment and the development of a competency profile for each individual involved.

6.0 Validate competency attainment procedures and assessment system

The purpose of this paper is not to propose a program evaluation model. The implication for total program assessment is made possible, however, by the program of competency based administrative development. The purpose of evaluation is to monitor the system and insure quality control. Competency development has immediate, short-term, and long-term consequences that require monitoring, and the expected consequences for each time span should be specified. Once performance attainment is measured, then the procedures for achieving competence can be assessed and revised. Whether a particular competency could best be acquired in the field rather than in formal course work, for example, could be better determined than it is currently. Finally, measures of performance in a competency based pre-service and on-the-job development program could be correlated with actual job performance.

UTILIZATION OF COMPETENCY ASSESSMENT

A systematic method for assessing competencies following these general parameters was utilized by Arizona State University in a 1976-77 project funded by the United States Office of Education. The following are the results, conclusions, and applications gleaned from this project. Specific findings allowed for an understanding of: (1) the ideal competency profile; (2) the level and source of competency attainment; and (3) the self-evaluation function of competency assessment (real profile).

Essentially, the analysis of the results of this project can be reduced to a description of data that allows for the development of several applications. These applications are: (1) performance assessment; (2) role definition and role conflict reduction; (3) program planning and need assessment; (4) research and development; and (5) certification assessment. Each application and its subsequent function is described below.

Performance Assessment

The need for objectives, valid instruments, and methods for assessment of performance on the job is well known. In teaching and administration of educational programs, assessment is a difficult and time-consuming task, and is often conducted in ways which are counterproductive to improvement of performance. Using the competency-based approach employed in this project, a sequence of steps was followed involving the role encumbent and those associated with that role. First, task areas were identified and statements descriptive of principal competencies were written. Next, indicators of each competency were specified. Third, competency statements were validated in the field. Fourth, those occupying the role responded to each competency statement described in the ideal, so that a generalized "ideal" profile for each of four roles was produced. Finally, each role encumbent did a self assessment (actual rating) of his or her own performance and compared it to the ideal.

Competencies rated and analyzed somewhat in this manner provide an objective, relatively emotion free, and data-based means of examining performance. From such analysis planned improvement, role conflict, and role clarification problems can be identified and expedited.

Role Definition and Clarification

The "ideal" profiles of competencies used in this project provided a means for defining and clarifying roles through the analysis of role expectations by various groups. In the project, teams of administrators from school districts met in sessions first as a group which shared similar roles, and then as individual district administrative teams. In this process, each role was examined and defined in competency terms and then reacted to by the administrative teams. In many cases, roles became defined specifically for the first time and many instances of potential conflict were identified. Role clarification became possible. After roles were defined in the ideal, it was possible to proceed to performance assessment which then verified the role definitions and permitted further clarification.

Need Assessment and Program Planning

The procedures employed in the project and the analysis provided serve as need assessment methodologies in two ways. First, within a district or school building, performance assessment using competency ratings became a means for assessing the in-service needs of personnel. The procedures used in this way relate in-service directly to validated performance standards. Successive performance assessments in turn provide a means of evaluating in-service training effectiveness so that in-service methods can be altered in terms of needs.

The project procedure is also applicable on a wider scale, and in fact, represents a means to conduct need assessment on a state-wide or regional basis. Competencies established and rated in the "ideal" can be rated across large groups in the "real" (actual). (See Figure 6-3.) These ratings of com-

QUADRANT ASSESSMENT MODEL AS A NEED ASSESSMENT DEVICE

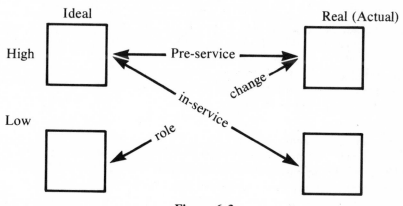

Figure 6-3

petencies cast in the matrix provided by the Quadrant Assessment Model provide listings of competencies in the categories shown above. High Ideal — High Real competencies can be assumed to be important competencies that are being performed in an adequate fashion by practitioners. Therefore, those being trained in pre-service programs should be able to perform adequately in terms of these competencies upon completing pre-service training. In effect, these competencies are important and anyone expecting to succeed should be able to perform them well. Hence, pre-service training, to be effective, should produce individuals ready to perform these competencies well.

Competencies in the High Ideal — Low Real category represent those which are important and which practitioners generally are not performing well. These competencies represent needs which can only be satisfied in in-service or continuing education programs. Those who would effectively improve practice in the field would need to attend to improving performance in these competencies.

Competencies in the Low Ideal — High Real category represent those which are of low importance but which are receiving undue treatment by practitioners. These competencies represent needs to alter role perception and to rearrange job requirements. Both pre-service and in-service education needs to attend to these competencies in terms of altering perceptions of the role and in changing role requirements.

Research and Development

The procedures carried out by the project represent means by which research might be undertaken in role definition, performance assessment, program planning, need assessment, and the like. Verification of results obtained, refinement of procedures, validation of effectiveness of the procedures are all legitimate areas of research. In addition, the QAM and the procedures for using it can play a significant role in research and development efforts. Competencies once identified and performance assessment conducted in this way lead: (1) to research and development required to design training programs; (2) to preparation and testing of materials for training; and (3) to design and testing of techniques for conflict resolution, role clarification, and trouble shooting.

Certification Assessment

Certification of professional personnel is an area in which dissatisfaction is generally acknowledged. Among reasons for dissatisfaction are: (1) that criteria are unrelated to ability to perform in professional roles for which certification is required; (2) that re-certification requirements do not provide a means for identifying incompetence; and (3) that certification does not take into account means of competence attainment other than formal course work.

Valid identification of competencies could free universities to provide training planned to promote those skills needed in performance in a professional role. Training and subsequent performance could be linked more directly to the realities of the field. Recertification, likewise, could be geared to performance assessment and training requirements identified by performance assessment. Much research and developmental work is needed in this area. The political questions surrounding certification must also be resolved. However, the QAM and the procedures piloted in this project represent a viable alternative to present certification requirements and procedures.

Some Possible Community Education Competencies

Results of the QAM as utilized in this project show some agreement on the competencies that ought to be exhibited by both district level and building level community educators.

At the district level it was noted that competencies should include: (1) defining policy through regulation development; (2) describing of budget information, including funding and costs; (3) identifying district-wide community education goals and objectives; (4) advising of unit coordinators regarding goals; (5) identifying resources; and (6) developing district-wide programs.

The competencies identified for building-level community education administrators were: (1) motivating participation in program; (2) recruiting community participation in overall program; (3) implementing programs; (4) promoting cooperation with the day shift; and (5) establishing and maintaining good relations with the district as a whole.

In general, it seems that the QAM is an excellent procedure for analyzing ideal community education competencies and for assisting community education staff to more closely approximate these competencies. ₊

REFERENCES

McCleary, L. E., & Brown, T. C. *Competency-based educational administration and applications to related fields.* Conference report presented at the Administration Competency Seminar; Tempe, Arizona (Arizona State University), 1973.

"In order to be effective, the leader must adjust his/her behavior to the particular set of circumstances and variables that comprise the situation in which the leadership is practiced." — Schmitt

Chapter 7

Appropriate Leadership Styles for the Community Educator

by
Donna M. Schmitt

APPROPRIATE LEADERSHIP STYLES
FOR THE COMMUNITY EDUCATOR

In a society where change is not only prevalent but continuous, it is natural to look to the basics in life to provide a steadying force. One of these basics is the social process of community. Indecision and confusion in social process is relieved when leadership is provided to help a group clarify goals and move toward the attainment of those goals. Perhaps this is one of the reasons why the concept of community education has been so readily accepted and has grown so rapidly in all parts of the country. The community education concept attempts to provide the educational leadership required to relieve the indecision and confusion resulting from the current societal malaise.

Citing the assumptions made by Minzey and LeTarte (1972), that communities do seek and are capable of positive change, that social problems have solutions, that one of the strongest forces for change is community power, and that community members are desirous of improving their communities, Seay and Associates (1974) state:

> Community education offers the best hope now visible in American society for developing these assumptions into foundations for sustained action upon complex societal problems. (p. 46)

This growing demand for leadership in community education makes it important that consideration be given to the influential factors in the training and developing of community education leaders, as well as to the effectiveness of these leaders once on the job. One of the most important of these factors is that of appropriate leadership styles, since these are the ways by which leadership behavior is expressed. Before discussion of these styles, however, it is necessary to review some pertinent literature in the area of leadership and leadership style.

Historically, there have been two major schools of thought regarding leadership theory: (1) trait theory; and (2) situational theory, including behavioral theory. The first was concerned with leadership as an attribute of the leader, or a combination of such attributes. The focus of this theory was on determination of characteristic traits of the leader from which his or her leadership behavior stemmed, regardless of the setting in which the behavior occurred. Research was conducted to determine the commonality of these traits, including personality factors, physical characteristics, and social background. Jenkins (1947), Bird (1940), and others attempted to correlate results of these studies, with less than conclusive results. Stogdill (1948) and Gibb (1954) both concluded that there seemed to be no consistent pattern of traits present in all leaders. Thus, as McGregor (1966) stated, "research findings to date suggest that it is more fruitful to consider leadership as a relationship between the leader and the situation than as a universal pattern of characteristics possessed by certain people" (p. 75).

The second major theoretical orientation to leadership research is the situational (behavioral) theory, which has, in turn, become the basis for much of the research'in the area of leadership style. The situational theory involves consideration of both the personality of the leader and the social setting in which he leads, that is, the unique combination of a particular leader functioning in a particular hierarchical organization (social system). Stogdill (1957, 1974) found that leadership was largely determined by the various components of the situation in which the leader was operating, and not as the effect of the sole influence of the leader himself. Thus it was that leadership behavior was analyzed according to two different patterns or subscales of behavior: (1) initiation of structure in interaction, which dealt with the building of relationships between the leader and the group members in areas of organization, communication, and methods of procedure, according to the group's task; and (2) consideration, which dealt with the building of relationships of trust and cooperation between the leader and group members (Hemphill, 1958). These two dimensions of leader behavior parallel the two goals of group functioning: (1) group achievement, or the group's striving to accomplish its task; and (2) group maintenance, or the group's striving to remain intact as a group (Halpin, 1966).

From the above, then, leadership is defined as multidimensional, as the performance of those acts which help the group achieve its objectives. These acts can be categorized as assisting in either of the two dimensions discussed, that is, as (1) acts which operationalize group achievement; or as (2) acts which help in group maintenance.

This definition of leadership forms the basis for analysis and definition of leadership style. Boles and Davenport (1975) state that leadership style is "a consistent manner in which an individual performs actions in helping a group move towards goals acceptable to its members" (p. 425). Getzels and Guba (1957) view leadership style as a function of both the nomothetic (institutional) and the idiographic (individual) dimensions of the leader's role in a social system. Other authors, such as Blake and Mouton (1964) and Blanchard and Hersey (1970) utilize the two dimensions of leader behavior defined by Hemphill (1958): (1) group achievement; and (2) group maintenance, and place these on a grid that allows for gradation and measurement of behaviors in each dimension. Variation in orientations or degrees of tendency in these measurements form the basis for distinctions in leadership styles. Thus, a leader could demonstrate a high degree of consideration of group achievement in his behavior without giving much indication of group maintenance, or *vice versa,* or both. (See Figure 7-1.)

TWO DIMENSIONS OF LEADERSHIP BEHAVIOR

Figure 7-1

Task Achievement

Reddin (1970) analyzed this two-dimensional measurement of leadership behavior with a third dimension of effectiveness superimposed. Thus, a leader may be found to be consistently demonstrating a behavior that is rich in consideration for the individuals of the group (group maintenance), and, at the same time, be giving little evidence of concern for achieving the goals of the organization (group achievement). This leadership style (behavior pattern) might or might not be exactly what is needed for the situation. Reddin (1970) indicates that if the behavior pattern is what is needed for the situation, it is effective; if not, it is ineffective. (See Figure 7-2.)

REDDIN'S THREE DIMENSIONS OF LEADERSHIP BEHAVIOR

Figure 7-2

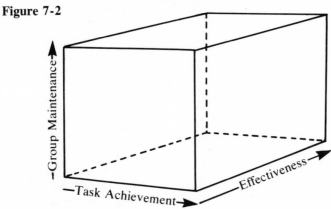

91

The significance of such an analysis is extremely important, since effectiveness is the very essence of leadership. It is also at the heart of community education, since the ultimate goal of community education is the self-actualization of the community.

What, then, can be said about effective community education leadership? Are there appropriate, as opposed to non-appropriate, leadership styles for the community educator? What conclusions can be gleaned from the literature?

It seems safe to say that there is no one leadership style that is appropriate for all community educators in all situations. Neither can it be held that there is one leadership style that is appropriate for a particular community educator in all situations. As was indicated by Cartwright and Zander (1958), McGregor (1960), and Stogdill (1974), leadership is a function of all the various personal, organizational, and social characteristics of each situation in which it is practiced. Thus, too, the leadership style utilized is particular to the situation. This is especially true for the community educator whose leadership must be practiced in many different settings and with many different individuals, as he or she attempts to self-actualize the community. Fiedler (1967) and Reddin (1970) both stress that in order to be effective, the leader must adjust his behavior to the particular set of circumstances and variables that comprise the situation in which the leadership is practiced. This skill to discern these variables and adjust leadership behavior accordingly is termed style flex by Reddin (1970). Obviously, style flex would be a necessary skill for the effective community educator.

This does not mean that there is nothing positively that can be generally stated regarding appropriate leadership styles specifically for community education. In a study involving superordinate and subordinate community educators, Schmitt (1975) noted that though there was a tendency for superordinates and subordinates to share a common leadership style after a period of time working together, it was far more prevalent for leadership styles to vary according to the setting in which each administrator worked. Thus, the community educator, most often the superordinate, who functioned as a member of the central office staff, was more often found to be exhibiting a high degree of task or group achievement behavior, while the community educator, most often the subordinate, who functioned in a local setting, as opposed to the centralized one, was more often found to be highly oriented in leader behavior toward group maintenance. Schmitt (1975) also noted that both groups were rated effective, indicating that effectiveness is dependent upon meeting the needs of the situation, and not in matching leadership styles of administrative teams. Here, again, conclusions regarding appropriate styles for community educators can be drawn. The task of the community educator is to help communities meet their needs and wants.

By definition, the community educator must be effective. Thus, selection of community educators for various roles should not be made on the basis of style match to pre-existing personnel, but on the basis of the individual's ability to exhibit style flex. Also, care should be taken not to conclude that because a community educator was effective in one situation, he or she will automatically be effective in another. This is often the fallacy upon which promotions from the field to the central staff is based. That such personnel are effective in their new roles is attributable to their ability to accurately perceive the leadership forces operative in the new setting and to adjust their leadership behaviors accordingly.

Underlying this entire discussion of leadership style and the community educator is the significant element of communication. The need for well-developed communication skills, both as a receiver and as a sender, for the effective community educator cannot be overemphasized. Everyone functions in a world of perceptions that may or may not accurately represent reality. This is especially true of the leader who, by reason of position, may be receiving faulty, or at least pre-screened, perceptions. The effectiveness of the community educator is directly related to accurate perceptions of the needs and resources of the community. This can only be the result of good communication skills coupled with the ability to accurately assess the leadership factors of the situation.

In summary, though there is no one specific leadership style that is appropriate for every community educator, there are leadership skills, such as communication skills, the ability to analyze and to synthesize, conceptual skills, technical skills, and human skills, that shape leadership styles which are effective for the varied situations confronting the community educator. It is necessary for that community educator to be trained in discerning the leadership elements in the situation and in responding with the most effective blend of task oriented and group maintenance oriented behaviors possible. This overall skill in style flex on the part of community educators will allow demonstration of the appropriate, particular leadership styles necessary to function effectively as leaders.

REFERENCES

Bird, C. *Social psychology*. New York: Appleton-Century, 1940.
Blake, R. R., & Mouton, J. S. *The managerial grid*. Houston: Gulf Publishing, 1964.

Blanchard, K. H., & Hersey, P. A leadership theory for educational administrators. *Education,* 1970, *90,* 303-310.

Boles, H. W., & Davenport, J. A. *Introduction to educational leadership.* New York: Harper & Row, 1975.

Cartwright, D., & Zander, A. (Eds.). *Group dynamics.* Evanston, Ill.: Row, Peterson & Co., 1958.

Fiedler, F. E. *A theory of leadership effectiveness.* New York: McGraw-Hill, 1967.

Getzels, J. W., & Guba, E. G. Social behavior and the administrative process. *School Review,* 1957, *65,* 423-441.

Gibb, C. A. Leadership. In G. Lindzey (Ed.), *Handbook of social psychology* (Vol. 2). Cambridge, Mass.: Addison-Wesley, 1954.

Halpin, A. W. *Theory and research in administration.* New York: Macmillan, 1966.

Hemphill, J. K. Administration as problem-solving. In A. W. Halpin (Ed.), *Administrative theory in education.* New York: Macmillan, 1958.

Jenkins, W. O. A review of leadership studies with particular reference to military problems. *Psychological Bulletin,* 1947, *44,* 54-79.

McGregor, D. *The human side of enterprise.* New York: McGraw-Hill, 1960.

McGregor, D. *Leadership and motivation.* Cambridge, Mass.: M.I.T. Press, 1966.

Minzey, J., & LeTarte, C. *Community education: From program to process.* Midland, Mich.: Pendell Publishing Co., 1972.

Reddin, W. J. *Managerial effectiveness.* New York: McGraw-Hill, 1970.

Schmitt, D. M. A comparison of the leadership styles of superordinate and subordinate community school directors in selected southwestern Michigan school districts (Doctoral dissertation, Western Michigan University, 1975). *Dissertation Abstracts International,* 1975, *36,* 654A-655A. (University Microfilms No. 75-18,058)

Seay, M. F., & Associates. *Community education: A developing concept.* Midland, Mich.: Pendell Publishing Co., 1974.

Stogdill, R. M. *Handbook of leadership.* New York: The Free Press, 1974.

Stogdill, R. M. *Leadership and structures of personal interaction.* Columbus: Bureau of Business Research, Ohio State University, 1957.

Stogdill, R. M. Personal factors associated with leadership: a survey of the literature. *Journal of Psychology,* 1948, *25,* 35-71.

"The education and training process for administration personnel must change if the desired ends of community education are to be met." — *Wilder*

Chapter 8

Administrative Roles in Community Education — the Superintendent, the Principal, the Director

by
Lawrence R. Wilder

ADMINISTRATIVE ROLES IN COMMUNITY EDUCATION —
THE SUPERINTENDENT, THE PRINCIPAL, THE DIRECTOR

Harold and June Shane, writing in *Learning for Tomorrow,* claim that in schools of the future "the community becomes a massive teaching aid and source of content. Implicit in the student-as-a-resource concept is the idea of the community as a resource, a teaching aid of vitality, an extensive school without walls" (p. 189). Community education has sought to achieve this end now, not tomorrow. By definition, "community education is the process that achieves a balance and a use of all institutional forces in the education of the people — all of the people — of the community" (Seay, 1974, p. 11). Education of this nature requires administrative skills often lacking in the normal training program. The concept need not change for the future, but the education and training process for administration personnel must change if the desired ends are to be met.

While many people and institutions fail to make a distinction between administration, management, and leadership, definite differences appear to exist. Boles and Seay (1974) establish different goals for administering and leading. Learning to solve common problems and maintaining the social system are the goals of administration while innovating, revising goals and meeting individuals' needs, are actions of leading. Management is basically the same as administration, but has been used more widely in the private sector than the public sector. With the advent of management by objectives and collective bargaining in the public sector, management is used more frequently in education. Both administration and management are involved with maintaining the organization. Leadership contains the seeds for change — innovation — toward predetermined goals. This writer believes that one can manage and administer without being a leader, but one cannot be a leader without performing management or administrative functions.

Webster's unabridged dictionary defines role as "a function performed by someone or something in a particular situation, process, or operation." Function becomes key to role accomplishment. The superintendent, the principal, and the director, all have administrative/management roles or functions to perform in community education.

Extensive work has been done with administrative or management functions. What might be termed a "general approach" to administration was first developed by Fayol, a French engineer turned administrator, in his book *Administration Industrielle et Generale* (1916). Fayol defined administration as "to plan, to organize, to command, to co-ordinate, and to control," and termed these behaviors the "elements of management." They have subsequently become known as "Fayol's Elements" and are delineated as follows:

> *To plan* means to study the future and arrange the plan of operations.
> *To organize* means to build up the material and human organization of the business, organizing both men and materials.
> *To command* means to make the staff do their work.
> *To co-ordinate* means to unite and correlate all activities.
> *To control* means to see that everything is done in accordance with the rules which have been laid down and the instructions which have been given. (Fayol, 1916, pp. 6, 43-110)

While each of these elements entailed more than his surface definitions, Fayol believed they were present in all business undertakings whether large or small, simple or complex. No matter where one was in the organizational hierarchy, each member performed these functions to varying degrees. As one ascended in the organizational structure, that member's ability to perform these functions became increasingly important. If all the functions were properly exercised throughout the organization, such an organization would be considered a successful operation.

In 1937 Gulick and Urwick co-edited *Papers on the Science of Administration* and built on Fayol's work. In response to the question, "What is the work of the chief executive? What does he do?" Gulick responded, "POSDCORB." These are the first letters of his expanded list of administrative functions — planning, organizing, staffing, directing, co-ordinating, reporting, and budgeting. Planning, organizing, and co-ordinating can be seen to have come directly from Fayol, while the command element would fall under Gulick's directing, with budgeting and reporting viewed as instruments of Fayol's planning and control.

Griffiths (1965) calls POSDCORB "an essential step which must be taken in the developmental path from art to science" (p. 26). Elsewhere he called this organization "the most widely known administrative taxonomy" resulting from an attempt to put all the functions of administration into a single table.

Writers have continued to expand these early concepts. Simon (1957) treated administrative functions and activities within a decision-making framework. Each of the functions delineated by his predecessors was examined in decisional terms.

More recently, Litchfield (1956) attempted to create a generalizable theory and saw the administrative process as: decision-making, programming, communicating, controlling, and reappraising. Additionally, Litchfield sought to show how the activities of administration were interdependent, that is, actually connected with how an individual or group handles the problem plus the activities of the entire organization.

The field of educational administration has drawn heavily from business. Sears (1950) listed administrative functions as planning, organizing, direction, coordination, and control. Ramseyer *et al.* (1955) are more elaborate, citing the functions of goal setting, policy making, roles determination, coordination of administrative functions, appraising of effectiveness, working with the community, leadership toward improvement of the resources of the community, involving people, and communicating. Decision-making, planning, organizing, communicating, influencing, coordinating, and evaluating were terms used by Gregg (1957). Others — Griffiths and Hemphill (1961), Campbell *et al.* (1962), and Grieder (1969) — deal with these traditional functions while Boles (1970) lists innovating, programming, and risk-taking. These latter seem to more directly approach the functions of the community school administrator, although all of the previous functions bear on the role of the superintendent, the principal, and the director in community education.

Eighteen administrative functions were gleaned by this writer (1975) for comparative purposes of traditional school principals and community school principals. These functions were evaluating, listening, planning, surveying, stimulating, controlling, decision-making, training, programming, communicating, innovating, directing, budgeting, leading groups, organizing, staffing, involving the community, and coordinating. With the help of a panel of experts these functions were determined to be human, technical, or conceptual skills, according to Weaver's (1968) definitions. Each of these functions become important to the administrative roles in community education.

THE ROLE OF THE SUPERINTENDENT — THE INNOVATOR

In spite of all attempts to spread the community education "gospel" many school boards and districts are not aware of the concept. The superintendent's role thus becomes that of an innovator. The district board must first be convinced that the community education concept is viable. As Sumption and Engstrom (1966) maintain, "the superintendent has the original responsibility of acquainting the board with the essential nature of school-community communication, pointing out its value to the community as well as to the school" (p. 135). This individual must use all of those skills which were determined to be human — listening, stimulating, communicating, leading groups, and involving community — in introducing the idea. Meetings must be conducted with the board, staff, and community leaders to "sell" the innovative plan of community education.

In addition to the human skills the superintendent must possess a high level ability in the conceptual skills area — planning, decision-making, innovating, organizing, and coordinating. Without a proper orchestration at this level, no music is developed.

As in business, the higher one is in the organizational structure, the greater the need for conceptual skills. This is especially true of the superintendent in community education because of the newness of the concept.

It becomes the responsibility of the chief school official to know the community education concept and communicate it to others. Many potential successes in community education have failed because full understanding and support was lacking at the highest levels in the school district. The superintendent's position must be occupied by an individual who has a strong commitment to community education if success is to be achieved in the implementation of the concept.

Many of the technical skills — evaluating, surveying, controlling, training, programming, directing, budgeting, and staffing — are delegated to either the principal or director of community education, thus allowing the superintendent time for the innovation aspects of the new program. However, it is imperative that some skill in these areas be possessed by the superintendent so that a supportive role to the principal and director may be played when needed.

THE ROLE OF THE PRINCIPAL — THE INITIATOR

Since the superintendent is the innovator, the principal becomes the initiator — the primary individual for determination of success at the building level. As Campbell (1969) states, "the chief school administrator is faced with peremptory commands — incredible in many instances — often mandates, that could dismantle management's role in education" (p. 42).

The role of the principal is often much like that of the superintendent, but operationalized in a smaller sphere. A great variety of human skills have to be used with the staff. Meetings — large and small — should be held to explain the concept of community education and answer any questions concerning its implementation. With constant, two-way communication, staff support should grow, making the principal's job easier.

In addition to working with staff, the principal must meet the community groups — service clubs, parents, church groups, etc. — to help foster the movement. The job becomes one of constant communications. Without community support, community education reverts merely to education.

While initiating a new concept, the principal must also continue the regular, day to day, functions of the school. A time should be established to meet with the community school director regularly. In the beginning phases of development these meetings should be frequent and long. Planning, organizing, deciding, budgeting, and coordinating, are most appropriate functions for these meetings. The principal has opportunity to share conerns and expectations with the director and understand what will be happening at the community's school, now no longer merely "his" school.

Further, the role of the principal is to "jell" the staff, the school, the community, and the program. More than likely, if the program fails, blame will be laid with the principal. Rather than merely allowing the director to operate without direction, the principal should supervise the director at least to some degree. Organizationally, the director should be accountable to the principal at the school site.

Many of the administrative or management skills — human, technical, or conceptual — performed by the superintendent are repeated with the principal. There is, however, a greater need for the technical and human skills at this level. Each principal must promote and nurture the growth of community education both philosophically and programatically. Without this active support, the concept will never achieve its potential.

THE ROLE OF THE DIRECTOR — THE IMPLEMENTOR

Someone has to implement the concept of community education, and this ultimate responsibility rests with the community school director. The superintendent and principal do have roles to perform, but theirs becomes a supportive function. With the necessary philosophical foundation in place, the director must now put the entire program together.

There must be a survey or needs assessment done with the community. A good director will seek to match the needs of the community with the resources of the community. Where needs exist for which there are not resources, the director, with the assistance of the community council, should seek to find or develop resources to meet the needs.

Once community needs are determined, the director must organize meetings, classes, exercises, etc., within the available facilities. Not all of these programs are necessarily held at school. Some may meet in churches, store fronts, fire stations or in other facilities made available for community use. There is no limit to the possibilities for meeting places. The key is to meet where the greatest number of community members can participate.

Ellis and Sperling (1973) pointed out the need for the director to be an organizer: "The most important of many tasks of the community school director is to organize the various constituencies in his community" (p. 55). This becomes a mammoth task, but one which must be accomplished if the role of the director is to be successfully implemented. Without this organization, important community leaders and groups may be missed, thus ultimately undermining the effectiveness of the program.

The roles of the superintendent, principal, and director, then, are interrelated, overlapping, and changing. There is, however, a great need for conceptual skills at the superintendent's level, for human skills at the principal's level, and for technical skills in the director's role. Obviously, these skills are not exclusive of each other, but must be performed to some degree by role encumbents at all levels. When each of these individuals fulfill their roles adequately and perform their functions appropriately, a successful community education program should be guaranteed.

REFERENCES

Boles, H. W. *Leaders, leading and leadership — a theory*. Unpublished paper, Western Michigan University, 1970.

Boles, H. W., & Seay, M. F. Community education leadership: a theory. In M. F. Seay (Ed.), *Community education: A developing concept*. Midland, Michigan: Pendell Publishing Co., 1974.

Campbell, C. M. The administration of community schools. In H. W. Hickey & C. Van Voorhees (Ed.), *The role of the school in community education*. Midland, Mich.: Pendell Publishing Co., 1969.

Campbell, R. F., Bridges, E. M., Corbally, J. E., Jr., Nystrand, R. O., & Ramseyer, J. A. *Introduction to educational administration* (4th ed.). Boston: Allyn and Bacon, Inc., 1971.

Ellis, P., & Sperling, J. The role of community school director as organizer. *Community Education Journal,* 1973. *3* (1), 55-56.

Fayol, H. [*Administration industrielle et generales*] (Starrs, trans.). London: Pitman & Sons, 1949.

Gregg, R. T. The administrative process. In R. F. Campbell & R. T. Gregg (Ed.), *Administrative behavior in education*. New York: Harper and Brothers, 1957.

Grieder, C., Pierce, T. M., & Jordon, K. F. *Public school administration* (3rd ed.). New York: Ronald Press, 1969.

Griffiths, D. E. Administration as decision-making. In A. W. Halpin (Ed.), *Administrative theory in education.* Chicago: Midwest Administration Center, the University of Chicago, 1958.

Griffiths, D. E., Hemphill, J. K., *et al. Administrative performance and personality.* New York: Columbia University Press, 1961.

Gulick, L., & Urwick, L. (Ed.). *Papers on the science of administration.* New York: Institute of Public Administration, 1937.

Litchfield, E. H. Notes on a general theory of administration. *Administrative Science Quarterly,* 1956, *1*(1), 3-29.

Ramseyer, J. A., Harnes, L. E., Pond, M. Z., & Wakefield, H. *Factors affecting educational administration.* Columbus: Ohio State University, 1955.

Sears, J. B. *The nature of the administrative process.* New York: McGraw Hill, 1950.

Seay, M. F. The community education concept — a definition. In M. F. Seay & Associates, *Community education: A developing concept.* Midland, Mich.: Pendell Publishing Co., 1974.

Shane, H. G., & Shane, J. G. Educating the youngest for tomorrow. In A. Toffler (Ed.), *Learning for tomorrow.* New York: Random House, 1974.

Simon, H. A. *Administrative behavior* (2nd ed.). New York: The Macmillan Co., 1957.

Sumption, M. R., & Engstrom, Y. *School-community relations.* New York: McGraw Hill, 1966.

Weaver, D. C. *Definitions.* Unpublished paper, Western Michigan University, 1968.

Wilder, L. R. A comparative study of functions performed by principals of community schools and principals of non-community schools (Doctoral dissertation, Western Michigan University, 1975). *Dissertation Abstracts International,* 1975, *36,* 1237A. (University Microfilms No. 75-19,570).

"More often than not, when Community Education fails to reach its potential, the leadership behaviors of the community educator in such situations can be found to be inappropriate to the setting or, at least, not perceived by others as appropriate to the setting." — Schmitt and Weaver

Chapter 9

Projecting a Professional Image — Appropriate Decorum For Community Educators

by
Donna M. Schmitt
and
Donald C. Weaver

PROJECTING A PROFESSIONAL IMAGE: APPROPRIATE DECORUM FOR COMMUNITY EDUCATORS

The philosophy of community education has been shown to be based upon sound educational theory and successful pedagogical practices in American educational history. The matching of community needs with community resources, and the delivery of human services to the community are, by their very nature, success-generating behaviors. If, then, the implementation of community education in a given community somehow fails to live up to expectations, the reasons for this failure must rest primarily in the human elements of the situation. More often than not, when community education fails to reach its potential, the leadership behaviors of the community educator in such situations can be found to be inappropriate to the setting, or at least not perceived by others as appropriate to the setting.

Thus, it seems important to the success of community education that community educators be perceived as leaders by those they are to to lead. This is the perceptual basis for leadership that Hollander (1964) addresses: "An individual's behavior is not only phenomenally present in interaction but is also subject to view and appraisal by the other members of the group" (p. 162). Perception does, in fact, shape reality. Certainly, the professional image projected by community educators is influenced by a number of factors discussed elsewhere in this publication — personality traits, political acumen, and leadership style — to name a few. However, equally important to the professional image of community educators is the exhibition of appropriate professional behaviors, the maintenance of professional decorum that is fitting to the leadership role expectations of those whom community educators are expected to lead. The perceived status of the community education leader by the group, then, is extremely influential in the success or failure of the leadership effort.

The basis for this perceptual view of leadership behavior is to be found in the concepts of status, role, and idiosyncrasy credit. Hollander (1964) indicates that status

> exists in the first place as a feature in someone's perceptual field, for without reference to a perceiver status has no intrinsic value or meaning in itself. And, similarly, role cannot be divorced from its perceptual locus; behavior is only appropriate to status insofar as someone perceives it to be so. (p. 167)

Status may then be considered to be the outcome of interactions whereby group leadership is earned after the leader has displayed appropriate behaviors. This means that the leader has not exhibited an excessive amount of unacceptable behaviors, and thus, has built up a bank of idiosyncrasy credit.

Historically, it would appear that there has been a conscious effort to play down the leadership role of community educators and to avoid behaviors which implied professional superiority. What community educators have accomplished as a result of their actions has been to reduce their "idiosyncrasy credit," and hence, their status among the very groups they are to lead as well as among other professionals.

No doubt, the prime reason for community educators to minimize their professional roles has been the interpretation of a number of educators that community education was an adjunct to the regular school program and, therefore, was not deserving of a status position within the education hierarchy. Another reason may be the desire of community educators themselves to disassociate themselves and their roles from the bureaucratic and impersonal aspects that may have characterized the past behaviors of the organizations and institutions with which they are affiliated. Further, there appears to be an understanding among community educators today that the "community" aspect is more important than the "education" aspect, and hence, that to be "with it" in the grass-roots community is more essential to the concept than to be a dedicated professional. Faced with this reality, community educators have opted for a low professional profile to avoid offending those whose cooperation is essential to the success of the community education effort.

It would seem that both the close affiliation with the community and the appropriate professional status of the educator are necessary to accomplish a viable model of community education. Knight (1971) has indicated that there is a strong positive relationship between professional status and task competency. To get the job done effectively, there must be an appropriate balance of professionalism, in the best sense of the word, and intimate knowledge of the community.

Thus, it behooves community education leaders who wish to be successful to examine those behaviors that would lessen their professional status. Actions by community educators which have resulted in unfavorable reactions to the community education movement include: (1) attempts to belittle the intellectual and evaluative roles within the movement: (2) behavior at local, state, and national meetings demonstrating greater concern for the social and recreational than for the professional aspects of the program; (3) efforts to thwart attempts to define the concept and develop theoretical models from which evaluation is possible; and (4) promotional campaigns using various techniques that treat community education as if it were a commodity to be hawked like a patent medicine at the county fair.

Such actions as those described above have resulted in a lessening of respect for the community educator and a consequent lowering of prestige for the movement generally.

The fact that most community educators are not deserving of such a reputation is little consolation to the 2,000 educators intent upon making a career of management and leadership in the field of community education. It is time that the profession examined that status of professional decorum among community educators in this country and dedicated itself to behaviors aimed at improving the professional image of leaders and managers within the community education movement.

How does one project a professional image as a community educator? The answer to the question of professional image implies a prior question, namely: What is involved in being professional? One of the writers had an opportunity to raise that question with Max Lerner, syndicated columnist, world-wide. The context within which Lerner was asked to respond involved the question of what makes a professional teacher. His reply was simple and direct: "There are primarily two factors involved in making the teacher a professional — authenticity and excitement." That is to say, professional teachers must be on the cutting edge of their profession, indeed, they should be contributing to current research and innovation in their field, and they must be able to excite others (the students) about developments in that field. So, too, with the community educator. Professional community educators contribute to research and innovation in the field of community education and support the research efforts of others in the field. Further, community educators utilize the results of research efforts to improve services to their clients. That is, community educators are authentic and as a result of that authenticity create excitement for the potential of the movement as it contributes to improving the quality of life in the community.

However, authenticity and excitement are not enough to insure a professional image for community educators. If community educators are to enjoy a reputation as professionals, they must be perceived by others as authentic and exciting. The projection of a professional image to others involves professional decorum on the part of community educators which is perceived by others as appropriate to their management and leadership roles.

What is professional decorum in this context? Professional decorum for community educators means simply behaving "in good taste," i.e., projecting by demonstrated behavior that which permits others to infer accurately what the community educator is about. It means authenticity and excitement personified in the behavioral sense. Professional decorum for the community educator implies behavior in support of the theoretical and evaluative phases of the movement as well as the practical, process aspects of the movement. It implies behaviors which represent the movement as a rational, empirical social action process requiring specialized skills and competencies rather than a mystical cure-all for the ills of society which can be directed by any well-intentioned, self-appointed leader.

Until those who call themselves community educators behave as if they believe that they represent a profession, there is little hope for the development of a professional image for the community educator.

What are the behaviors implied in the development of a professional image for the community educator?

Authenticity. To be viewed as authentic requires of community educators certain behaviors perceived as appropriate by others both inside and outside the profession. Community educators who are judged to be authentic are likely to demonstrate by their behavior that they:
1. Are on the cutting edge of their discipline — they are involved in testing ideas and producing new and useful information.
2. Are politically astute, but do not play politics, i.e., they are aware of the political ramifications of their actions, but do not make decisions based upon personal political advantage.
3. Are able to separate their personal assessment of the individual from their professional evaluation of his/her performance.
4. Operate from a supportable theory of community education and are involved in testing the hypotheses emanating from that theory.
5. Do what they say they will do and do not make promises they are incapable of fulfilling.
6. Keep strictly to themselves all information provided in confidence.
7. Avoid accepting assignments requiring expertise which they do not possess, i.e., refusing to demonstrate the Peter Principle in community education.
8. Are sensitive to situations requiring their services and make themselves available to serve when the need for their services is evident.
9. Meet time deadlines including appointments, meetings, and filing of reports.

Excitement. The professional image of community educators depends, in part, upon how dedicated they are perceived to be or, to put it in Lerner's terms, how much excitement they are able to generate in support of the concept. Community educators who are perceived as exciting are likely to demonstrate by their behavior that they:
1. Believe that community education can improve the quality of life within the community.
2. Care what happens to people and communities, i.e., they evaluate

their work in terms of tasks accomplished rather than amount of time and effort expended.

3. Believe that the function of leadership is to help others to reach *their* goals.

4. Are willing to be perceived as humble, even at times naive, in order to serve the interests and needs of others — probably listening more than initiating conversation.

5. Are able to utilize a variety of leadership styles depending upon the situation.

6. Demonstrate concern for people's problems beyond merely verbalizing it, i.e., they are able to initiate structure to solve problems for people.

7. Become significant others to those with whom they work.

8. Are influential within the system in accomplishing the goals of community education.

9. Resist the temptation to become advocates for particular causes. This generates a win-lose situation that results in rifts in the community, rather than in an emphasis of common concerns and common goals.

In summary, if community education leaders are to be considered professionally *authentic* and *exciting,* certain decorous behaviors are required; for it is upon the basis of observation of these behaviors by those within the profession that those outside the profession form judgments regarding what the profession is all about. Community educators would do well to ponder their own codes from which decorum derives so that their outward behavior may reflect an inner commitment to a set of principles worthy of professional emulation by those aspiring to the profession. Community educators ought to exhibit behaviors that do not sell themselves and their profession short.

REFERENCES

Hollander, E. P. *Leaders, groups, and influence.* New York: Oxford University Press, 1964.

Knight, B. M. A study of selected variables associated with idiosyncrasy credit (Doctoral dissertation, Western Michigan University, 1971). *Dissertation Abstracts International,* 1971, 32, 2957A. (University Microfilms No. 71-30, 019)

PART III

THE ARENA IN WHICH COMMUNITY EDUCATION IS PRACTICED

"That there have been profound changes in the American social setting in recent years which make it difficult to identify "community" is apparent to most community educators. What may not be so apparent are the facts that earlier criteria applied to community may no longer be useful, and that alternative ways of viewing community may be required if we are to continue to develop viable programs and processes which serve present-day American society." — Weaver

Chapter 10

Making Sense Out Of Community

by

Donald C. Weaver

MAKING SENSE OUT OF COMMUNITY

INTRODUCTION

A universally accepted goal of community education is an increased "sense of community." To reach that goal involves a number of intermediate objectives including assessing community interests and needs, identifying community resources and power points, and involving community members in joint planning efforts by means of a community council or similar representative body.

An examination of recent writing and research in the field of community education reveals considerable dissatisfaction with our efforts to accomplish the intermediate objectives implied in reaching the ultimate goal of increased sense of community (National Community Education Association, 1975). Community interest and need assessments often fail to elicit community-wide response and are, therefore, considered to be unrepresentative samples. Efforts to identify community resources and power points often result in conflicting goals and thus failure to respond. Community councils are frequently unable to act as a result of their failure to muster a quorum of the membership for the meeting (Lind, 1975; Myrdal, 1974; Seay, 1974; Warren, 1963).

Can such failures be attributed to sinister forces at work deliberately attempting to sabotage efforts of community educators to develop a sense of community? Or, worse yet, can it be that humankind no longer recognizes a need for community? Neither seems likely. Rather, it would appear that failures of community educators to accomplish their objectives in terms of processing result from a misconception of what constitutes "community" within present-day American society and, hence, an inability to apply effective techniques for developing a sense of community.

WHAT IS COMMUNITY?

That there have been profound changes in the American social setting in recent years which make it difficult to identify "community" is apparent to community educators. What may *not* be so apparent are the facts that earlier criteria applied to community may no longer be useful, and that alternative ways of viewing community may be required if we are to continue to develop viable programs and processes which serve present-day American society.

Much of the literature in community education, as well as much of the practice, is based upon an assumption that "community" is a physical

117

aggregate of individuals in a particular place. Such a definition of community is a convenient one for the community educator inasmuch as (1) it delineates clearly the constituency he/she is to serve; (2) the logistics of needs assessment are simplified because of limitations within geographical boundaries; and (3) representation to the community council can simply be based upon a particular geographical area such as an elementary school catchment area. Aside from the convenience, however, the concept of community as a place is probably of little use to the community educator in most American towns and cities today because there appears to be little relationship between where one lives and the "communities" with which he or she is associated. As Keyes (1975) pointed out, "Most of us in city and suburb live one place and find 'community' in another" (p. 9). Hence, limiting definitions of community to a particular geographical area may well prevent the community educator from serving constituencies presumed to benefit from the presence of a community education program.

Most students of community appear to agree that there are three ways to identify community.

(1) People holding things in common — property, ideas, beliefs, customs, norms, sentiments, or activities.

Such a criterion applied to community makes possible the identification of a social community, a church community, a fraternal community, and an academic community to name a few. Communities based upon the criterion of things held in common usually involve a commitment by the individual to the group (community), and a sustained membership in the particular community so long as the individual is viewed as committed to that which is held in common.

(2) People operating within certain social-systems and sub-systems where if one part behaves in a certain way other parts will be affected in a predictable manner.

Applied to community, this criterion makes possible the identification of community systems such as the family system, the educational system, the economic system, and the class system. Further, having identified the social system, the community educator can identify sub-systems, and analyze the dynamics of the interrelationships between and among systems and sub-systems. For example, having identified education as a social system it is possible to identify and analyze relationships among such sub-systems as (1) the board of education, (2) the central office staff, (3) the teacher's union, (4) the staff of a particular school, (5) the student body of the school, and (6) cliques within the student body of the school.

(3) People occupying particular land or territory.

This criterion for identifying community, when associated with the first two criteria, can be useful in a particular geographic area. However, as indicated earlier, this criterion does not pertain to most urban and suburban settings today, and probably applies to only a limited number of rural areas where choice of community is restricted by geography.

Although not empirically tested and obviously not endorsed by scholars in the field of community, a fourth criterion for identifying community is posited for consideration.

(4) People enjoying a tentative commitment to each other — that is, a community of transients.

Such a criterion makes possible the identification of communities which, unlike the other forms of community, make only short-term commitments either out of necessity or by choice. This kind of community can be built on a tour bus, in a hotel bar, a shopping center, or a commune.

During a recent visit to Guam, the writer was struck by the tentative tenure of much of the population living there. The characteristic greeting is "How long will you be here?" Yet even among these people, many of whose lives of necessity have been characterized by transiency, it is possible to detect a desire for "community." Further, there appear to be a growing number of Americans who, if given a preference, would choose a community of transients because of the freedom it provides — that is, they would choose what Keyes (1975) called "a place where it's safe to be known" — but not too well! Although they may not desire relationships involving long-term commitments, they do, nevertheless, seek "community."

Since the present patterns of living among most Americans are such that the concept of community as a specific geographical area is obsolete, no attempt will be made to examine the notion of people occupying a particular territory as a viable criterion upon which to base a community education program. Rather, three criteria, namely, things held in common, social systems, and transitory commitment will be discussed as means of identifying and analyzing community for the purpose of developing a sense of community. However, before discussing each of the criteria for identifying and analyzing community, some discussion of the goal we are trying to reach is in order.

THE GOAL — A SENSE OF COMMUNITY

No doubt, most community educators would agree that the ultimate goal of community education is to develop "a sense of community." And one gets the impression that what most of us have in mind when we say "sense of community" is a kind of idealized version of the home town where everyone knows everyone else and altruism prevails. However, given the existing conditions in most American communities today, a return to the "home town community" seems not only unrealistic but downright impossible. Yet, most community educators are committed to the efficacy of the concept of community and, therefore, believe that some progress is possible in the direction of improved quality of life within the towns, villages, and cities of America. Progress toward the improvement of community life requires that we have some notion regarding what conditions prevail when we have achieved "a sense of community." Although there are, no doubt, indicators of a sense of community in addition to those listed below, the writer believes that the following conditions would be observed in most areas which could be said to have achieved a sense of community:

1. An organizational structure through which collective action involving two or more systems and/or sub-systems is achieved.

2. The presence of a super-coordinating agency which promotes analysis of common area problems and coordinates involvement from all major community systems in the resolution of those problems.

3. Opportunity for each individual to have membership in and commitment to several communities in which he/she is known and accepted.

4. Substantive involvement of citizens in all major agencies and institutions in the area.

5. Evidence of adoption of social norms and constraints appropriate to the area.

6. Commitment to life-long learning — opportunity for adults to pursue educational endeavors that result in the implicit realization that there exists a society outside their own private worlds.

7. Evidence that the area is committed to a two-way responsibility for education — a school which provides leadership and encouragement for adults to continue their education and a neighborhood which provides school-age children with realistic community exposure.

8. Communication across boundaries of systems and sub-systems — interaction between communities of interest.

9. Superordinate goals which are impossible to reach without cooperation across social system boundaries.

10. Evidence of accommodation and mediation within and across di-

verse and conflicting social systems — detente among communities of interest.

11. Access to reliable information and data required for the study and resolution of social and environmental problems.

12. Access to state and national systems through which solutions to problems originating outside the local area can be effected.

COMMUNITY IS WHERE YOU FIND IT

It must be borne in mind that in most villages, towns, and cities in America today *community is where one finds it*. That is to say, modern communication and transportation make it possible to seek community wherever groups of common interest can be found. Such a range of choices means that few people are limited to their immediate neighborhoods in their selection of communities with which to join. Voluntary memberships in service clubs, church groups, hobby clubs, and recreation centers often require travel of several miles from one's place of residence. Similarly, many people by virtue of their business or profession are automatically members of social systems that provide a broad array of social and recreational outlets which take them out of their neighborhoods for most, if not all, of their community activities. Further, either out of necessity or choice, many people seek tentative community involvements — communities characterized by short-term itinerant relationships. Here, too, most of such communities are outside the neighborhood in which the person resides. Many people must travel extensively and move frequently as part of their business and professional obligations. Such people must, of necessity, seek community where they can find it — the airport, the hotel, the bar, the laundromat, or the shopping center. Similarly, those who seek tentative communities by choice, prefer that such communities be outside their local neighborhoods to permit greater freedom and less commitment to the community. Such people want to be known and accepted by the group, but this acceptance to be based upon only a tentative commitment to and tenure in the group.

That the neighborhood elementary school is an important locus of community interest cannot be denied. That it is only one of many foci of community interest in present-day America must also be readily admitted. To the extent that it represents a viable locus of community interest, the neighborhood elementary school should be utilized. However, community educators would be well advised to open themselves to *all* potentialities for the promotion of a sense of community including, but not limited to, the neighborhood elementary school.

Further, since community is based upon commonality of interest and identifiable social systems, attempts to identify and analyze community membership and function must take cognizance of the fact that in any geographical area there are probably *many communities,* and that most residents of the area probably belong to more than one community. Hence, community educators who purport to study the dynamics of community must deal with *many communities and numerous social systems* and sub-systems, as well as the interrelationships among those communities, systems, and sub-systems.

COMMUNITY EDUCATION — DEVELOPING A SENSE OF COMMUNITY

Assuming that the ten conditions cited earlier represent at least partial evidence that a sense of community exists, there follows an examination of how the criteria for identifying and analyzing community relate to reaching the goals implied in a sense of community. Despite the need to be aware of the various "communities" discussed earlier, there are usually geographical and/or political boundaries which identify the area to be serviced by the community educator. Hence, efforts to assess the presence of a sense of community must of necessity take cognizance of a geographical area or neighborhood.

Organizational Structure

The first condition observed in an area which has achieved a sense of community is an organizational structure through which collective action is achieved. James Coleman (1966) in a chapter entitled "Community Disorganization" said:

Social organization is important for one reason alone: to enable the social unit to take action as a unit. If bridges are to be built, wars won, food grown, criminals caught, then there must be organization . . . If a community can act collectively toward the problems that face it, then it is well organized. If it cannot, then it is disorganized relative to these problems, though there may be a great amount of apparent organization. (p. 672)

The goal of community education is an "organized" community — one which, despite self-interest among separate social systems, can, when the common good demands, take collective action. Collective action is achieved with a minimum of organizational effort in groups described by Ferdinand Tonnies (Coleman, 1966) as *Gemeinschaft* (characterized by strong identification with others and sympathy among the members). Such a close identification and commitment is likely to be present in small rural communities, where members are associated over a period of time and strong bonds of mutual friendship and loyalty exist. However, most community educators operate in areas representative of what Tonnies (Coleman, 1966) described as *Gesellschaft* (characterized by strong self-interest and the absence of mutual identification). The challenge to the community educator in this situation is the development of an organizational structure through which collective action can be achieved despite the lack of mutual identification and sympathy.

Efforts to establish an organizational structure capable of promoting collective action among diverse interests requires:

1. A thorough knowledge of the social systems and sub-systems operating within the area and the particular self-interests represented by the respective social systems and sub-systems.
2. Acquaintance with the opinion leaders within each social system and their sub-systems.
3. Sustained contact with representatives of each social system and sub-system in the area by means of a community council or other representative body.

The hope for collective action among diverse communities of interest lies in capitalizing upon what Coleman has called "mutual self-interest." Although the examination of the alternatives available for promoting community organization are beyond the scope of this discussion, the reader interested in pursuing this subject is referred to Coleman's (1966) treatment of "community disorganization" (p. 670-722).

One further point is relevant. The tendency to comprise the community council on the basis of mutual interest may well be a mistake for two reasons. First, such a basis of representation often does not identify a referent group — an issue to be discussed later. Second, and more germane to the development of a structure for collective action in the presence of conflicting self-interests is the fact that such conflicting interests must be represented at the council table if conflict is to be attenuated. Mutual admiration societies are comfortable groups with which to associate, but they do not provide a setting for resolving conflict and moving toward the resolution of problems of the larger community. Community educators would be well advised to comprise community councils to include all communities of conflicting self-interest.

A Coordinating Agency

The accomplishment of the first condition, namely, an organizational structure through which collective action is achieved, is dependent upon the second — *the presence of a super-coordinating agency which promotes analysis of common area problems, and coordinates citizen involvement from all major community systems in the resolution of those problems.* Whether such an agency is sponsored by the school or some other institution is of little consequence. What is of concern to the community educator is that such a coordinating agency is operative in the area, that its functions are well publicized and supported, that the educational system with all its sub-systems is actively involved, and that leadership to carry out the functions of the coordinating agency is trained and supported in its endeavors. Indeed, liaison with such an agency is an important part of the job of the community educator, for the success of education as a social system is dependent upon the viability of other social systems with which it is associated.

Membership in Several Communities

The third condition to be found in an area which has attained a sense of community is *the opportunity for each individual to have membership in, and commitment to, several communities in which he or she is known and accepted.* Freedom of choice is a prime requisite in a democractic society. So, too, is a broad choice among communities a requirement for residents of an area which boasts a sense of commmunity. Such opportunities are par-ticularly crucial at a time in our development as a nation when we no longer must devote prime attention to making a living and can devote a major portion of our time to social, political, and recreational pursuits. Sociologist Daniel Bell (1973), in *The Coming of the Post Industrial Society,* discussed at length the social problems which result from the affluence created by our present economic successes. It is in an effort to attenuate these social prob-lems that the community educator attempts to provide opportunities for membership in a variety of communities.

Americans are known as a society of joiners, and there are justifiable reasons for this reputation, both social and psychological. Yet, fewer than half the people in the United States belong to voluntary associations outside those to which they automatically hold membership by virtue of their rela-tionship with the social system of the workplace. Of particular concern to the community educator are those persons who seek community but are unable to find it. A wide variety of opportunities should be provided for membership in two kinds of voluntary communities: (1) those permitting commitment over a sustained period of time; and (2) those involving short-term, transitory commitments.

Organizations of the first type are common in most areas as the roster of any active community education program will reveal. However, efforts to provide community of the second type are not so prevalent and, yet, may be equally important in a society characterized by what sociologist Ralph Keyes (1975) has called mobility, privacy, and convenience. In an article in the *National Elementary School Journal* (1975), Keyes wrote:

> Mobility is a major enemy of the community of intimate friendship. But I'm not clear where it is cause and where effect — whether we're afraid to get moving on, or whether we're always moving on because we're afraid to get close. (p. 10)

Whether cause or effect, many present-day Americans appear to crave tentative community — community of a short-term, transitory nature. Such a need is nowhere more evident than in hotels and motels catering to traveling businessmen. The writer recently spent an evening in a motel lounge conversing with four men — two national sales representatives for large manufacturing companies, one an itinerant legal counselor, and the fourth a government employee. All of these men spend five days of each week away from their home neighborhoods. The five of us voluntarily formed a group to meet a need for "community." On another occasion, while teaching in a college in Australia, the writer was approached by a group of students who wished to form a community which, according to the spokesman, was for the purpose "just to talk." When the writer asked "why with me?" the response was, "You will soon be moving on and we're free to discuss things with you." In other words, the encounter would provide the need for stimulation and fellowship while providing sufficient anonymity to make it safe to join the group. There is a great unexplored potential for leadership by community educators in the development of tentative communities — in hotels, bars, educational institutions and, yes, even shopping centers. Two new shopping centers in the Detroit area provide beautiful accommodations, anticipating the services of community developers who can organize tentative communities utilizing such facilities.

Communities based upon short-term, transitory need or desire may have a further advantage that should not be overlooked. Most communities form naturally around common interests and concerns within particular social systems. That is, social sub-systems are likely to develop within the larger business, religious, or educational systems within the area. For example, it is common for educators to depend almost exclusively upon sub-systems within the educational system for their social activity. While such groups have the obvious advantage of homogeneity, they often tend to be provincial in nature and function and, therefore, provide little incentive for one to broaden contacts outside his particular social system. On the other hand, communities based upon short-term, transitory needs are probably more likely to develop across social system boundaries and, hence, tend to be less provincial in nature and outlook. The community formed in the motel lounge described earlier is a case in point. This transitory community was comprised of five men, represented diverse interests, and discussed many of the substantive social and economic issues of our time. Although this discussion group represented a very tentative commitment to community (four hours), it did involve an interchange across several social system boundaries. Engaging in social intercourse with those outside one's profession or business provides an opportunity to experience the diverse points of view represented within an egalitarian society. Forming communities across social system boundaries may open the way for understanding and acceptance among those of diverse interests and backgrounds — a condition required if we are to achieve sense of community within the larger community of mankind.

Citizen Involvement in Public Affairs

In addition to the apparent need for opportunities for community through voluntary social and recreational groups, there is a current demand for *substantive involvement by citizens in policy deliberations of all major agencies and institutions in the neighborhood* — a fourth condition upon which to judge the presence of a sense of community. Political scientist Alden Lind (1975), in an article entitled "The Future of Citizen Involvement" appearing in *The Futurist,* documented what he believed to be a growing alienation from political institutions by the American public. Lind proposed 18 modes of citizen involvement aimed at restoring trust and confidence. The modes suggested ranged from vouchers, surveys, and ombudsmen to neighborhood resource centers, community development corporations, and public hearings. Since space does not permit discussion of the modes for citizen involvement here, community educators are urged to examine Lind's recommendations with a view toward improved citizen involvement. Community educators must give particular attention to involvement modes which apply to the educational system and sub-systems. It is through these organizations that the community educator has the opportunity to demonstrate exemplary involvement modes to be modeled by other community agencies and institutions.

Social Norms and Constraints

A fifth condition required for a sense of community is evidence of the adoption of social norms and constraints appropriate to the area. There is conflicting evidence regarding whether or not community education contributes directly to the improvement of social conditions within the community. However, despite evidence or lack of it regarding the direct impact of community education upon social norms and constraints, it is to be expected that community education would be utilized as the process through which the particular area deals with social problems. Hence, where a sense of community is said to exist, one would expect to find cooperative efforts to control behavior in accordance with what is considered appropriate in that community.

Commitment to Lifelong Learning

A demonstrated commitment to lifelong learning characterizes the sixth criterion for the development of sense of community. Historically, in the minds of most people education and schooling have been considered synonymous; hence, for most Americans, education is perceived to begin at age 5 and end at the completion of high school or college. However, recent efforts in adult education and community education have convinced large numbers of people that one never ceases to learn and that, therefore, learning activities whether under the sponsorship of the school or other community agencies are appropriate at any stage in one's life. Seth Spaulding (1974), in a paper prepared for the Institut de Sciences Jouridiques du Developpement of the Universite de Paris, proposed that to provide the wide variety of learning activities appropriate for all members of the area requires program range as illustrated in Table 10-1.

Table 10-1

RANGE OF LIFELONG EDUCATIONAL SERVICES AND ACTIVITIES

TYPE VI:	Services which provide a broad range of informational and educational media from which people select according to their interests; although there may be structured services linked to other educational programmes, most cater to serving a broad spectrum of individual interests.
EXAMPLES:	Television; radio; magazines; newspapers; libraries; bookstores; newsstands; information centres; etc.
TYPE V:	Participant-governed groups in which people elect to join in activities with others of similar interests; programmes often include seminars, courses, and speakers, but such formal activities are secondary to the basic goals of the group.
EXAMPLES:	Youth organizations; political clubs and organizations; social groups and clubs; service clubs and organizations (Rotary, etc.); labour organizations; co-operative organizations; religious groups and institutions.
TYPE IV:	Loosely structured educational services which seek to find and influence people with a fairly prescriptive message and content; people can elect to listen or participate if they wish; often seek to encourage other groups and services to assist in spreading the message.

Table 10-1 — *Continued*

EXAMPLES:	Agricultural extension services; consumer education; health education services; land-reform education programmes; community-development education ("social education" in India); on-the-job training schemes; "animation" (French); population education; environmental education; consumer education.
TYPE III:	Moderately structured educational activities and institutions usually consisting of formal courses and seminars directed toward prescriptive learning goals.
EXAMPLES:	Community centres; self-learning centres; work-study schemes; correspondence education; "university-without-walls" (USA); open university (UK and elsewhere); teachers' centres (especially UK); armed forces training schemes; career education (USA); farmer training; adult basic education (USA); functional literacy (UNESCO); folk high schools (Scandinavia); manpower training (USA); "job corps" (USA).
TYPE II:	Highly structured and prescriptive educational activities with long-term goals, but involving a degree of flexibility in organization and programme.
EXAMPLES:	Alternative schools (UK and USA); multi-unit schools; individually prescribed instruction schools; comprehensive schools, etc.
TYPE I:	Highly structured and rigid educational institutions and programmes with a highly prescriptive content.
EXAMPLES:	Traditionally structured elementary, secondary, technical, and higher educational institutions.

Source: Spaulding, 1974, p. 103.

In other words, demonstrated commitment to lifelong learning requires activities ranging all the way from highly structured program and content such as that provided by the school for those of compulsory school age, to optional and unstructured opportunities based upon interest, and without restrictions of age or previous educational experience.

Most community educators are well aware of the wide range of adult education opportunities offered under headings such as skill building, recreation, and enrichment. What we may be missing in the process of providing for lifelong learning are two objectives proposed by Benjamin DeMott (1975) in a discussion of the philosophy of continuing education in *Saturday Review*. DeMott, while supporting the type of continuing education activity referred to above, suggested two possible objectives not usually considered by those developing skill building, recreation, and enrichment programs. The first is related to the improvement of the inner self:

> Mid-life learners often do open themselves to their own variousness, extending and altering their modes of response to the world. (p. 28)

The second possible objective of continuing education according to DeMott is related to the improvement of a sense of community:

> A class or a course helps a person rediscover the essential as opposed to the accidental humanness. And that act equips us anew for participation in the larger society, by winning from us an implicit recognition that a society larger than our private world does exist. (p. 28)

Obviously, some educational experiences are more likely to result in "altering modes of response to the world," and "recognition that a society larger than our own private world does exist" (p. 28). What those experiences are remains a challenge for the community educator. However, perhaps an even greater challenge lies in evaluating both existing and newly developed programs of adult education, not on the basis of whether or not they pass local bond issues or reduce vandalism, but rather on the basis of whether or not they result in a belief on the part of the participant that he has changed in some significant way with respect to perception of self or of others.

Two-Way Responsibility for Education — School and Community

An area which has developed a sense of community provides opportunities for lifelong learning as indicated above, but, more than that, provides opportunity for school-age children to have realistic community exposures — i.e., it *demonstrates a two-way responsibility for education between school and community* — a seventh condition of sense of community. Adults decry the lack of social responsibility on the part of young people today; yet, few opportunities exist for the young to experience the problems of the society outside the textbook and the classroom. Internships and community study projects are two of many such opportunities by which the community can provide a real sense of community to young people.

Interaction Between Communities of Interest

Optimum growth and development of any social system requires that the system be *open* — i.e., that it has input from other social systems. At a time characterized by efforts on the part of powerful education lobbies to *close* the educational system to outside intervention, it is encouraging to observe efforts on the part of some areas committed to a sense of community to *provide communication across boundaries of systems and sub-systems — interaction between communities of interest.* The school as a social system should be open to input from the major social systems and sub-systems within the area — parent organizations, student groups, service clubs, government agencies, political organizations, etc. Similarly, these systems should seek reciprocal arrangements with the school if a sense of community is to be a reality. Community educators must be students of the social system and be perceptive regarding opportunities to open communication both within each social system, and across the boundaries of all social systems within the area.

Superordinate Goals

In the absence of a sense of community each social system is likely to pursue its own objectives — often at the expense of the goals of others. Sense of community requires the *presence of superordinate goals which are impossible to reach without cooperation across social system boundaries.* Nearly every issue of the *Community Education Journal* is replete with examples of community commitment to projects representing superordinate goals and descriptions of the processes which are employed in bringing such projects to fruition. Most accounts of such projects stress joint planning and cooperative activities. This condition, namely, *cooperative effort to accomplish goals which transcend particular social systems,* may well be the ultimate test of the success of the community education effort. Each social system has strong motivations to accomplish its own purposes, but what is often required is sublimation of single-system objectives to accomplish a goal which is community-wide in scope and purpose. The area which is served by a well-organized community education program is likely to depend upon personnel assigned to the program for leadership to coordinate joint efforts toward accomplishment of superordinate goals. In such cases the area is likely to evaluate the success of the community educator based upon how well he or she performs in this role.

Detente Among Communities of Interest

The accomplishment of superordinate goals requires still another condition related to the development of a sense of community, namely, *accommodation and mediation within and across diverse and often conflicting social systems — detente among communities of interest.* If there is hope for the resolution of the social and environmental problems facing local areas, states, and the developed nations of the world, including the United States, such accommodation and mediation are imperative. Biologist Charles Birch

(1975) detailed in simple, non-technical language the consequences of man's blind, unplanned progress in an age of explosive growth and technological development. The following are a few of Birch's well-documented observations:

> Those of us who count ourselves amongst the affluent could ask ourselves what right we have to use such a disproportionately large share of the earth's resources. The affluent countries represent twenty per cent of mankind but they consume ninety per cent of the earth's resources that are consumed each year, and that proportion is growing. This is the biggest moral issue that the limits to growth raise for affluent countries. It raises awkward questions about distributive justice in the world. Whose upward aspirations for material growth must first be checked? Where are restraints to be put? What is to be reduced — the luxuries of the rich or the necessities of the poor? What are the priorities — decent human environment for the whole human species or riches for some and squalor for the majority? (pp. 35-36)

> The first report to the Club of Rome in 1972, *The Limits to Growth,* was a tour de force in bringing home to many people the indisputable yet unappreciated fact that the earth is finite. Because the earth is finite, because of the exponential growth of people, of use of the earth's resources and of environmental deterioration, we came to see for the first time that we are fast moving from an age of resource abundance to one of resource shortage. To continue on this path at the rate we are going, argued *The Limits of Growth,* is to head for disaster. We cannot expect technology to save us. (p. 42)

> The current crises in energy, food, inflation and unemployment are not just temporary flashes in the pan. They reflect persistent trends inherent in the present pathway of uncoordinated growth and development. (p. 78)

It would seem that the resolution of such social and environmental problems as those cited by Birch require both political action and education. Ultimately, such problems will require political action at the local, state, national, and international levels. However, before political decisions are possible, politicians must have the support of an enlightened citizenry which is aware of the severity of the problems, is committed to the need for action to resolve such problems, and is prepared to accept the consequences of alternative solutions. In other words, area-wide educational programs may well be similar to those recommended by Toffler in *Future Shock* (1970) when he proposed that each local community should have "councils of the future" where such problems could be examined (p. 358). Birch (1975) proposed a similar grass roots approach to the educational aspects of the problem:

The sustainable society is a revolutionary concept. It will not be achieved without revolutionary political transformations involving the demise of power groups with interests vested in the status quo. It will be a struggle against enormous odds, but not a struggle of one elite group against another. The struggle begins and must be maintained at the grass roots level amongst people. It will be in villages and towns and schools and universities and political groups, and wherever small cohesive groups of people can become full participants in decision making. (p. 26)

With encouragement and support from the World Future Society several efforts to develop such grass roots processes are already underway in the states of Hawaii, North Carolina, and Washington.

The prime contribution of community education in the years immediately ahead may well be in the area of promoting cooperation across social system boundaries in order to develop grass roots processes aimed at the study of such future problems as the environment, population growth, world resources, and human relations. Obviously, such efforts will be fraught with controversy, and will require a state of detente among existing social systems within the local area. That is, selfish interests may have to accommodate and mediate where superordinate goals of survival are concerned. *The alert community educator will take advantage of every opportunity to promote accommodation and mediation across social system boundaries to insure both a sense of community and a future for all of mankind.*

Access to Reliable Information and Data

To deal adequately with the problems cited above, as well as others facing local areas, will require access to reliable information and data for decision-making at the local level. Even though Toffler (1970) contended that the success of local councils depends upon leadership at the grass roots level, he conceded that there will be need for the services of "specialists," many of whom it is assumed must come from outside the local area. Similarly, even though information will be disseminated by the local media, much of the basic data regarding such technical matters as environmental and population control must come from technically competent sources outside the local area. Community members are likely to seek assistance from the community educator in locating technical resources appropriate to the matters under consideration by local councils, and to give direction regarding proper use of outside technical resources at the local level.

Access to State and National Systems

In the highly complex American societal structure nearly every social system at the local level is part of a super structure organized at the state and national levels. The local educators belong to state and national education associations, the county medical society is a branch of a state and national medical association, the local union is affiliated with state and national labor organizations, etc. Where a sense of community prevails, local social systems capitalize upon their state and national hierarchies to supply valuable information and services to the benefit of the local area.

Furthermore, in cases where policy decisions at higher levels control local social system operation, it is often a necessity that those committed to a sense of community at the local level bring pressure for change higher up in the system. Community educators must at times admonish those exerting control within local systems to communicate needs and expectations to those in policy-making positions within the social system hierarchy in order that all local systems may participate in reaching the superordinate goals of the local area.

SUMMARY

During the past 35 years the community education movement has developed a reputation for providing programs and processes which help people to achieve a sense of community. And the societal malaise evidenced in most American communities today emphasizes a need for continued efforts toward the development of community during the next 35 years. It is to be hoped that the community education movement will continue to be a viable force for cooperation among all social systems in the direction of achieving a realistic sense of community in the neighborhoods of America.

In the past, efforts to achieve a sense of community have been geared primarily to the needs and desires of local neighborhoods — particularly elementary school catchment areas. However, the living styles of most Americans in towns, cities, and suburbs today forebode a totally different approach to community in the future — one which transcends the local neighborhood. Rather than viewing community as a place, the community educator may now need to think of community in terms of commonality of interest within particular social systems. Such a universalistic view of community coupled with the growing recognition that education is a lifelong process not restricted to schooling, per se, may require re-thinking what constitutes both "community" and "education."

The writer has proposed a definition of community based upon common interests within social systems, and has applied that definition to a set of 12 conditions present in an area which may be said to have achieved a sense of community. Whether or not one accepts either the proposed definition of community or the conditions considered essential to achieving a sense of community is of little consequence. What is of concern is the need for every community educator to re-examine his or her definition of community taking into account the living styles among present-day Americans, and the need to develop programs and processes appropriate to achieving a realistic sense of community among diverse and conflicting social systems.

REFERENCES

Bell, D. *The coming of the post industrial society*. New York: Basic Books, 1973.

Birch, C. *Confronting the future*. Ringwood, Victoria, Australia: Penguin Books, 1975.

Coleman, J. Community disorganization. In R. K. Merton & R. A. Nisbett (Eds.), *Contemporary social problems*. New York: Harcourt Brace, 1966.

DeMott, B. Adult education — The ultimate goal. *Saturday Review,* September 20, 1975, pp. 27-29.

Keyes, R. In search of community. *National Elementary Principal,* January-February 1975, pp. 9-17.

Lind, A. The future of citizen involvement. *The Futurist,* December 1975, pp. 315-328.

Myrdal, G. Mass passivity in America. *The Center Magazine,* March-April 1974, pp. 72-75.

National Community Education Association. *Community education research monograph: Issues and answers*. Ann Arbor: University of Michigan, Office of Community Education Research, 1975.

National Community Education Association. *Community education research monograph: Issues and answers*. Ann Arbor: University of Michigan, Office of Community Education Research, 1976.

Seay, M. *Community education — A developing concept*. Midland, Mich.: Pendell Publishing Co., 1974.

Spaulding, S. Life-long education: A modest model for planning and research. *Comparative Education,* June 1974, pp. 101-113.

Toffler, A. *Future shock*. New York: Random House, 1970.

Warren, R. L. *The community in America*. Chicago: Rand McNally, 1963.

*"Community education provides a systematic method for relating in-
stitutions, for bridging the gaps between these social systems and institutions by reaching back and forth across boundaries and institutional barriers, for identifying needs as well as resources, for applying resources from
one system or institution to problem solution in another, and thus for improving the quality of life for the entire set of social systems called the
community . . ." — Schmitt*

Chapter 11

Social Systems —
Application to Community Education

by
Donna M. Schmitt

SOCIAL SYSTEMS — APPLICATION TO COMMUNITY EDUCATION

As a concept and a philosophy, community education has captured the imagination and idealism of an ever-increasing number of educators and professionals, as well as the lay citizens and the grassroots community members who constitute the heart of society. The community education concept holds the promise of new strategies for expediting both old and new problems. Philosophically, community education synthesizes what seems to be the best of many previously-tried solutions and welds them into a new and potentially far more effective force. At the core of community education's potential for delivery lies its utilization of the power of institutions and social systems.

Social systems are a natural development of the nature of mankind to group together in order to achieve common objectives more expeditiously (Jay, 1971). Social bonds of interrelatedness are built up over a period of time; dependencies and interdependencies are formulated as groups attempt to achieve goals. Ultimately, a whole series of formal and informal networks of communication and behavior develop that can generally be termed social systems.

Boles and Davenport (1975) more specifically define a social system as "a group of persons in which the action of one affects the actions of others" (p. 426). Social systems, however, are abstractions, and thus, not visible nor accountable per se. Rather, social systems are operationalized through the institutions which seek to give permanence to various human values. Further, social systems themselves become intertwined in the individual lives of the persons who move through and within various social systems on a day-to-day basis. Schematically, these interwoven social systems might appear as in Figure 11-1.

SOCIAL SYSTEMS' INTERACTION

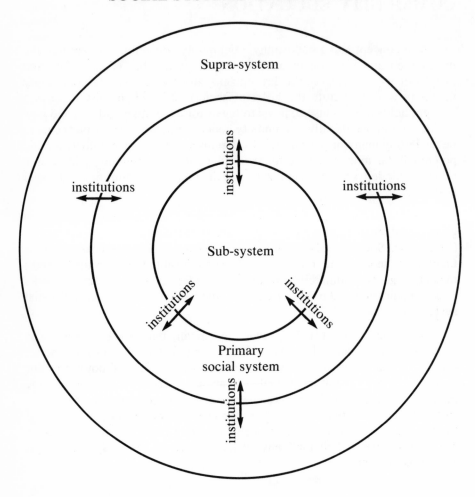

Figure 11-1

Thus, it is the individual who moves within and through social systems by means of various institutions that provide the unifying force in social systems' theory.

Analysis of the operational definition of the *system* part of social system is the key to the understanding of the application and significance of community education theory. The *system* approach is generally defined to mean that there is *input,* which is acted upon by some *process,* resulting in a new entity, called an *output.* (See Figure 11-2.)

THE COMPONENTS OF A SYSTEM

INPUT ───────────────▶ PROCESS ───────────────▶ OUTPUT

Figure 11-2

Application of this schema to the theory of community education indicates that community education's input is two-fold: (a) the needs and problems of the community; and (b) the resources of the community. The process of community education is its catalytic, energizing function (Minzey, 1974) that synthesizes the input in such a way as to: (a) minimize the forces of the needs and problems of the community; and (b) maximize the potentials of the resources of the community. This results in the two-fold output of community education, that community problems are solved through: (a) meeting of needs; and (b) utilization of resources. (See Figure 11-3.)

ILLUSTRATION OF
COMMUNITY EDUCATION AS A SYSTEM

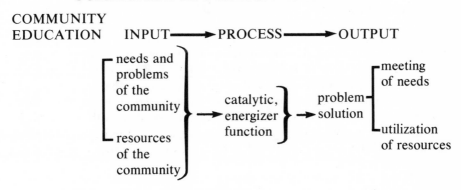

Figure 11-3

It is most important to note here that one of the most powerful aspects of community education is that the above *system*-atic process is operationalized through existing institutions. This allows for the indigenous resources of various institutions, such as public schools, agencies, and governmental bodies, to be developed and ordered in such a way as to provide for planned, but nonetheless effective, change. Utilizing existing institutional structures also reduces risk and enhances what Berger and Neuhaus (1977) call "mediation" for communities.

> Such mediation cannot be sporadic and occasional; it must be institutionalized in *structures*. The structures . . . have demonstrated a great capacity for adapting and innovating under changing conditions. Most important, they exist where people are, and that is where sound public policy should always begin. (p. 4)

The key, then, to the inner working of community education in relationship to social systems is that community education is a system for managing human problems, which system has been given permanence and direction by being seated in human institutions, primarily the public school, but in others as well. It is necessary that both of these factors be recognized, for a system without a structure to give it permanence is quickly dissipated, and an institution without a viable operational process is lifeless. As Alinsky (1971) states:

> We must never forget that so long as there is no opportunity or method to make changes, it is senseless to get people agitated or angry, leaving them no course of action except to blow their tops. (p. 118)

It is essential that ideas and change have institutions to operationalize them in an orderly fashion.

As noted above, individuals dwell in a world of interrelated systems (see Figure 11-1), bridged by institutions. Often, however, these institutions themselves have little or no effective interaction. This results in lack of communication, multiplication, and magnification of problems, neglect of resources, and duplication of programs. Even more serious is the confusion, mistrust, and despair of the individuals who try to deal with all of these institutions in various systems in a rationally and aesthetically satisfying manner, and who consequently suffer from loss of the ability to cope with life.

Community education provides a systematic method for relating institutions, for bridging the gaps between these social systems and institutions by reaching back and forth across boundaries and institutional barriers, for identifying needs as well as resources, for applying resources from one system or institution to problem solution in another, and thus for improving the quality of life for the entire set of social systems called the community and for the individuals in each community.

Real education is the means by which the membership will begin to make sense out of their relationship as individuals to the organization and to the world they live in, so that they can make informed and intelligent judgments. (Alinsky, 1971, p. 124)

This, in effect, is the synthesizing function of community education. It is this function and its resulting community benefits that is the unique product delivered by community education when analyzed in a social system setting.

REFERENCES

Alinsky, S. D. *Rules for radicals*. New York: Random House, 1971.

Berger, P. L., & Neuhaus, R. J. *To empower people*. Washington, D.C.: American Enterprise Institute for Public Policy Research, 1977.

Boles, H. W., & Davenport, J. A. *Introduction to educational leadership*. New York: Harper & Row, 1975.

Jay, A. *Corporation man*. New York: Random House, 1971.

Minzey, J. D. Community education: another perception. *Community Education Journal*, 1974, *4* (7), 58-61.

"Whether working at the neighborhood level or in a geographic area containing diverse neighborhoods, the community educator may often find it necessary to identify aggregations of people with similar needs and preferences, hereafter called constituencies. *A community educator, as a leader, has the task of bringing these constituencies to agreement on the level of preferences to be delivered and then into action."* — *Oravecz*

Chapter 12

Constituency Building and the Politics of Community Education

by
Michael T. Oravecz

CONSTITUENCY BUILDING AND THE POLITICS OF COMMUNITY EDUCATION

Community councils and advisory councils have been advocated as methods by which community educators can identify the needs and preferences of members of their communities. Even when these organizations are properly formed and utilized the community educator may find that the needs and preferences identified do not strike a responsive chord with significant numbers of people. Such lack of response may result in the offering of courses for which not enough people enroll, or the identification of a community problem which interests the members of the community council but which community members themselves treat with apathy. When this occurs, the community educator experiences some degree of frustration and wonders what went wrong. Why haven't the people responded?

One possible answer is dependent upon understanding a set of assumptions common to the application of economics to political phenomena. The assumptions are those of scarcity, methodological individualism, self-interest, and individual rationality in the use of scarce public goods and services — i.e., "goods or services that when provided are available to everyone, and one person's consumption of them does not reduce the consumption of others" (Bish and Nourse, 1975, p. 20).

By scarcity it is meant that individuals desire more goods and services than are available. Thus, they must choose among available goods and services and decide how much they are willing to contribute for any additional goods or services. The contribution may be in various forms including taxes, fees, individual time spent, or exchanging a service they can provide for one they desire.

Assuming the individual to be the basic unit for analysis constitutes the assumption of methodological individualism. With this assumption, society and organizations are viewed as interactions inherent or essential to individuals, not as something that exists apart from individuals. The individual is considered the primary unit of analysis, not the organization.

The assumption of self-interest is that "individuals undertake actions because they stand to benefit from them" (Bish, 1971, p. 5). It is important to understand that this assumption does not imply that people are necessarily selfish. It is recognized that individuals perform actions for more than material gain. The benefit they accrue may take the form of love, honor, or some other intangible of which they may not even be aware. However, no matter what the reason is, individuals choose courses of action which will benefit them.

Lastly, the assumption of individual rationality means that, where choices of action are involved, "an individual will choose the course that he feels will give him the greatest satisfaction" (Bish, 1971, p. 5). This assumption is necessary because "it would be impossible to predict human behavior without it" (Bish, 1971, p. 5). The term individual rationality which means the community places alternatives in order "according to its collective preferences once for all, and then chooses in any given case that alternative among those actually available which stands highest on this list" (Arrow, 1963, p. 2).

Herein lies the problem. By using community councils and other such organizational methods to determine individual preferences, logical consistency has been expected from an organizational-choice process that combines individual preferences and "no generally accepted assumption in economic or democratic theory indicates that organizational rationality in an organic sense should be expected where individuals are the unit of analysis" (Bish, 1971, pp. 506). That is, an organizational-choice process does not necessarily measure individual preferences because each is made for different reasons.

The previous observation does not invalidate the concepts of community councils and advisory councils, for collective action is recognized as necessary to achieving the efficient allocation of public goods and services. However, two things must be considered. The first is that "any individual would achieve the highest level of satisfaction if his tastes were identical to the median tastes in the political unit of which he forms a part" (Bish, 1971, p. 49). Secondly, "apparently, individuals with similar tastes for public goods live in the same neighborhoods" (Bish, 1971, p. 49). Therefore, a community council more effectively measures individual preferences when it is organized at the neighborhood level — a practice advocated by Minzey and others in the field of community education.

However, even within the same neighborhood there is no reason to expect all individuals to have the same preferences for public goods and services. Whether working at the neighborhood level or in a geographic area containing diverse neighborhoods, the community educator may often find it necessary to identify aggregations of people with similar needs or preferences, hereafter called *constituencies*. A community educator, as a leader, has the task of bringing these constituencies to agreement on the level of preferences to be delivered with the members of the various constituencies and should establish credibility among them, especially if he is new to the community and is likely to be viewed as an "outsider."

As a way of familiarizing himself with and building credibility among people in the community, it is recommended that a community educator engage in a political process called *constituency building*. Constituency building consists of activities that take a community educator out of his office and into the community where people live, work, and recreate. Its purposes are: 1) to enable a community educator to become better acquainted with the members of a community in order that he can gain a broader perspective regarding their preferences; and 2) to enable the members of the community to become better acquainted with him and the purpose of his job so that he has increased credibility among them, thus, making it easier for a community educator to mold the people into various constituencies needed in order to meet the identified preferences.

There are many kinds of constituency building activities. In fact, the list of activities in which a community educator could engage is limited only by his imagination. The important thing to remember is that most constituency building activities should be conducted away from the office, with the objective of becoming better acquainted with people and their needs and preferences rather than attempting to influence them on an issue or a set of issues.

Constituency building calls for a combination of certain leadership capabilities and personal characteristics. First, and perhaps foremost, a community educator must be a good listener. As Burke (1969) pointed out, listening involves more than just hearing. It is an active process requiring a person to interact with the speaker in order to ferret out the main idea from the speaker's message. Furthermore, listening is made more effective when, in addition to understanding the speaker's perspective, the listener tries to find the speaker's frame of reference. This is an empathic process which requires the listener's "attempting to experience the same feeling about the subject as the speaker" (Burke, 1969, p. 75).

Also, a community educator engaged in the process of constituency building should listen to everyone. This means that there has to be a willingness on his part to accept people for their individuality and their opinions. A community educator should remind himself, as Alec Thompson, the central character in a novel by McGee and Moore (1976), keeps reminding himself:

> You had to listen, even to the fools. When you quit listening, you lost touch with reality, and began to live in that dangerous intellectual world of logic and reason unleavened by stupidity and irrationality. (p. 10)

A willingness to listen to what people have to say is not a trivial thing. This attitude results in an openness on the part of individuals in the community which, in turn, results in a free-flowing contribution of ideas, and good ideas often come from the least expected sources.

Lilenthal (1967) has identified characteristics that he perceives as being essential to what he calls the humanistic manager-leader. Included in his list of characteristics are a willingness to take into account the public's opinion, and the ability to induce the public not only to agreement but to action, that is, to build a constituency. Further, the humanistic manager must be able to recognize the point at which people are ready to act. Lastly, such a manager sees qualities and capacities in people that they themselves can not see.

These same characteristics and abilities are needed by the constituency builder. The importance of the willingness to take into account the public's opinion has been discussed along with the topic of listening and, therefore, requires no further elaboration. The ability to induce the public to agreement and to action is needed so agreement on the level and method of delivery of identified needs and preferences can be reached. However, being able to induce people to action is different from being able to recognize the point at which people are ready to act. The community educator must be like the good salesperson who knows when to close a deal. If he is not, even though agreement has been reached as to the level of preference and method of delivery, the people may still not respond because the timing is inappropriate.

Through the ability to see qualities and capacities in people that they can not see in themselves, the community educator maximizes the utilization of the talents and energies of people in order to lessen delivery costs of needs and preferences. Earlier it was pointed out that the scarcity of public goods and services requires individuals to decide how much they are willing to contribute for additional goods and services. People are frequently unaware that they possess a talent or a skill that they can exchange for a need or preference. Such contributions are important because they also reduce the delivery cost to other individuals having the same preference, thus increasing the probability of satisfying more people.

The prime role of the community educator is leadership. It seems reasonable to assume that successful leadership requires clarity of direction. In community education, that direction comes from the leader's constituency — the community. All community organizations, including the community council, are utilized to build a constituency to support the agreed upon direction. The astute community education leader builds a constituency to support the direction in which he leads for, without it, he may no longer be the leader.

REFERENCES

Arrow, K. J. *Social choice and individual values* (2nd ed.). New York: John Wiley and Sons, 1963.

Bish, R. L. *The public economy of metropolitan areas.* Chicago: Rand McNally College Publishing, 1971.

Bish, R. L., & Nourse, H. O. *Urban economics and policy analysis.* New York: McGraw-Hill, 1975.

Burke, W. W. Interpersonal communication. In W. B. Eddy (Ed.), *Behavioral science and the manager's role.* Washington, D. C.: NTL Institute for Applied Science, 1969.

Lilenthal, D. E. *Management: A humanist art.* Lectures presented at the 1966 Benjamin F. Fairless Memorial Lectures, Carnegie Institute of Technology. New York: Columbia University Press, 1967.

McGhee, E., & Moore, R. *The Chinese ultimatum.* New York: Pinnacle Books, 1976.

Minzey, J. D. & LeTarte, C. *Community education: From program to process.* Midland, Michigan: Pendell Publishing, 1972.

Seay, M. F., & Associates. *Community education: A developing concept.* Midland, Michigan: Pendell Publishing 1974.

PART IV

STRATEGIES FOR COMMUNITY EDUCATION LEADERSHIP

"Community involvement must utilize a combination of vehicles, not relying upon simply one means." — *Parson*

Chapter 13

Involvement Strategies In Community Education

by
Steve R. Parson

INVOLVEMENT STRATEGIES IN COMMUNITY EDUCATION

The literature of community education has always placed abundant emphasis on community involvement. The philosophy of the movement has always been based on the concept of people becoming involved in a process of identifying their own problems, and then bringing the resources of the community to bear on these problems in a coordinated fashion.

Article after article has been published about the means to achieve community involvement through community advisory councils, community surveys, public hearings, and many more. However, after all the rhetoric about community involvement, community educators admit privately that community involvement really is not happening in their communities. They are usually quick to add that they are working on it and soon people in their community will be meaningfully involved.

Many questions spring to mind. What is it these community people are going to be involved in? How are they to be involved and to what extent are they to be involved?

"Community involvement" seems to be the term with which community educators have identified, whereas people in other fields lean more toward "citizen participation." These terms will be used in this paper interchangeably to refer to the same process.

A noted consultant in the field of citizen participation strategies, Sherry Arnstein (1969) has written that " . . . the idea of citizen participation is a little like eating spinach: no one is against it in principle because it is good for you" (p. 216).

Many find spinach eating very difficult even though it is known to be nutritionally good. Likewise many community educators know that community involvement is good, but have a great deal of difficulty making it work.

Whether the admission is palatable or not, what is really being discussed under the guise of community involvement is citizen power. In its fullest sense it is a redistribution of power which enables a wide scope of people to join in the political process in the community. It is the strategy by which the "have nots" join in determining how goals and policies are set, resources are allocated, and programs are operated. The problem, as Arnstein (1969) points out, is that there " . . . is a critical difference between going through the empty ritual of participation and having the real power needed to affect the outcome of the process" (p. 216). Involvement or participation without the redistribution of power is a frustrating process for the powerless. What sometimes happens is that people find they have *particpated in participation,* which is often a meaningless way professionals use to meet the mandates of involvement.

The process of community involvement has many variables. These variables include: 1) the commitment of the institution; 2) the ability of the staff to work effectively with the community; 3)leadership development and support given the community; and 4) the vehicles provided for involvement. This article will focus on the latter, vehicles for involvement, with no intention of diminishing the importance of the other variables.

VEHICLES FOR COMMUNITY INVOLVEMENT

The impact of the Watergate incident served to awaken this country to the crisis of trust and confidence in American institutions. Numerous nationwide public opinion polls have shown a strong feeling that the quality of life in America has deteriorated. The polls also showed a growing percentage of people who feel isolated from things going on around them, and an alarmingly large percentage of people indicate that what they think does not mean much any more.

According to Lind (1975) our society is experiencing a revolution of rising expectations. In the past, rising expectations have related to material things, like automobiles, homes, etc. But today

the expectations focus on the level of trust and mutual esteem in human relations. We have, fundamentally, a political revolution — an exploding demand by citizens for significant involvement in an expanded political life. (p. 317)

Institutions must face this "political revolution" with a commitment to develop new vehicles for involving the community. Community involvement must also utilize a combination of vehicles, not relying upon simply one means.

No attempt will be made here to explore in depth all of various vehicles that have been developed in recent years. However, several modes of involvement are highlighted to encourage the reader to consider an array of alternatives.

1. *Advisory Councils, Boards, and Committees —*
Without question this has been the most widely used mode of involvement in the field of education. The authority given to these groups range from strictly advisory, as in most community school councils, to total control, as seen in some of the decentralized

neighborhood school boards. Unfortunately, many professionals are not well prepared to work with community groups, and little attention has been given to helping citizens acquire skills to become effective participants.

2. *Surveys —*
A wide variety of survey techniques have been used to provide short-term feedback. Some localities (New York City; Roanoke, Virginia) combined television with mailed ballots sent in by the public.

Community surveys are often fraught with sampling problems. It is difficult to reach all segments of a community and obtain totally unbiased data. Surveys do, however, provide an efficient means of getting input from a large number of citizens.

3. *Public Hearings —*
Public hearings tend to be used for special purposes such as rapid community input. Hearings are held regarding public institution budgets, capital improvement projects, and long-range plans. Because of the lack of other vehicles for obtaining involvement, the public hearing appears to be used with increasing frequency by a wide range of agencies, institutions and levels of government. Public hearings, according to Lind (1975), "often produce hostility and enmity where none is necessary. More often than not, the only people who leave happy are the idle spectators" (p. 319).

4. *Community Resource Centers —*
Community Resource Centers, rather new on the scene, are considered part of what is currently being called the community self-help movement. As defined by the National Self-Help Resource Center (1976), a Community Resource Center is

> an opportunity — for people to learn how to serve themselves. It is a place to recycle our resources, to get in touch with people, to provide fair and thorough information about community issues, to ask for and act on citizen opinion. It is a place to exchange information, develop community dialogue and build coalitions to resolve community problems. (p. 1)

These centers operate much like a community school, but are generally located outside the bounds of traditional institutions, and often without a professional staff. In fact, one of the most striking characteristics of those involved in self-help projects is a distrust of professionals (Back and Taylor, 1976).

5. *Ombudsmen* —

In several localities ombudsmen have been established for both schools and local government. Ombudsmen are basically citizen representatives who will trace individual citizen problems through the system toward resolution. The ombudsmen respond to a wide variety of problems and inquiries, and can assist individual citizens in resolving problems or, at the very least, in getting the problem heard.

6. *Community Development Corporations* —

The general purpose for these corporations is to provide a legal, non-profit body for projects which may not enjoy the approval of a sufficient number of political influentials to obtain significant government support. The attitude of local governments or school boards toward these groups has often been one of indifference or peaceful coexistence. Some Community Development Corporations have been formed to implement and operate community education programs where the public schools or local government have not wanted to provide the necessary leadership.

7. *Games and Simulations* —

Several games and simulations have been devised to assist citizens in developing their roles as participants in the process of community education and community development. One simulation, "Manleyville" (Porter, 1974) is designed specifically to be used within the framework of a community education program. Simulations help citizens see the community development process in its entirety.

8. *Block Clubs* —

The use of Block Clubs is generally the result of a felt need to increase the accessibility of the participatory process (Shafer, 1974). Block Clubs provide a small intimate group atmosphere where citizens can become involved with a very low level of threat. The groups often meet in homes in the neighborhood over coffee. This model, unfortunately, tends to involve primarily females and often only parents of school-age children. However, Block Clubs are frequently able to deal with a wide range of community concerns.

9. *Citizen Evaluations* —

Institutions, agencies and units of government are becoming acutely aware of the need for evaluation in this age of public accountability. In the process of developing an effective evaluation process, some have included a form of citizen evaluation. The models for citizen evaluation range from a very traditional information gathering and review process to trial by a jury made up of citizens. In the trial model, presently in developmental stages at the Northwest Center for Community Education, the University of Oregon, advocate and adversary roles are played out in courtroom fashion. The advocate presents evidence and witnesses to establish the value of the program. The opposition counters to establish a case for curtailment or reduction of the program. This model offers some exciting potential for dramatically involving the community in the process of evaluation as jurors, witnesses, and evidence gatherers.

10. *Conferences* —
Conference models of two different types have emerged as techniques to add dimension to community involvement: 1) special issue conferences; and 2) general forum conferences. The special issue conferences have attempted to bring together citizens to discuss and study particular issues, such as the environment, roles of women in society, and energy. The general forum conferences have become quite popular during the Bicentennial era, as many communities held Townhall meetings to discuss general issues of concern. These meetings were held in big cities and small towns throughout the country with varying degrees of success.

11. *Community Expositions and Exhibits* —
One of the commonly heard comments about community involvement is that so many people are not aware of all the resources that are available to them in their community. In rural Gloucester County, Virginia, the Community Education program sponsored a "Community Expo." Over 80 community agencies were represented by means of demonstrations, service, and information. Several thousand people came together to participate in what was the country's first attempt at large scale community involvement. Participants in expositions of this type can be asked to provide community agencies with input on needs for programs and services.

Upon reviewing these various involvement strategies, it is important to note the tendency of agencies and institutions to adopt one single strategy for involvement with little regard to its appropriateness. There is a great danger in limiting involvement to one single mode. Because of some of the weaknesses inherent in each vehicle, it would appear that a multi-faceted approach to community involvement would allow one strategy to offset the weaknesses of another.

MALPRACTICE IN COMMUNITY WORK

At the risk of making a rather abrupt shift, the author would like to turn to a topic that should be of interest to all professionals involved in community work, malpractice. The issue of malpractice is raised in this discussion of community involvement strategies to attempt to focus some attention on the undercurrents which lie below the issue of involvement.

There is a general awareness of the concern in the medical profession over malpractice. Lawsuits against physicians are growing in numbers, and the size of the financial judgments are also escalating in alarming proportions. But how many of us have given any thought to malpractice in community work?

Warden (1977) in a recent paper reasons that since malpractice is defined as any misconduct or improper performance in *any* professional or official position, then no one group has a monopoly on malpractice. Warden continues that this means that community educators, as well as other professionals, have the potential to engage in malpractice.

In developing the idea of malpractice on community work, Warden (1977) poses the following thought-provoking questions:

Who is the community worker's client?

Under what circumstances can malpractice be attributed to the individual worker's fault, a sponsoring agency's, or the community?

Can community members file a lawsuit?

To what extent can a community worker be held accountable for the actions of others?

How can we measure the impact of the worker on others?

To whom is a community worker really responsible?

What happens with regard to conflict between professional values and community values? (p. 6)

Since these questions are just beginning to emerge, it is obvious that there are few answers. At the heart of many of these problems is the desire on the part of community workers to exercise personal power and nurse their own egos. Research by Bailey (1973) has also indicated that community workers spend a disproportionate share of their time on issues and conditions which have a high personal value to them even though community members may have other high priorities.

Institutions come in for their share of criticism as well. Warren (1973) suggests that "when an institution functions primarily to enhance its own welfare and growth, it is certain in the end to jeopardize the interest of the community as a whole" (p. 166).

Warden (1977) also applies the possibility of malpractice to community education by identifying some potential malpractice areas.

Initiating efforts with little or no knowledge and/or involvement from the community.

. . . Encouraging people involvement in schools and other agencies without consideration as to specific ways/processes of such involvement.

Implementing an organizational model or plan that is consistent with national trends but inconsistent with local community conditions.

Developing leadership patterns which lead to the dominance of hired personnel.

Developing operational procedures which are inflexible.

Undertaking 'empire building' on the part of individuals and organizations.

Forming advisory councils without thought as to their purpose and responsibilities. (p. 9-10)

There should be a definite commitment on the part of community education professionals to continually reassess practices in light of the responsibility to serve the community. Opportunities must be provided for people to assess their community and to determine where it should go and what it should become. Without this goal attempts to utilize strategies for community involvement are futile and without meaning. As Carl Marburger (1976) has stated:

The message to school people is what we've been finding and feeling across the country — parents want to be involved. But creating new advisory councils won't solve problems in itself. Public involvement is valuable only when those in power want it to be. (p. 8)

REFERENCE

Arnstein, S. R. Eight rungs on the ladder of citizen participation. *Journal of the American Institute of Planners.* 1969, *35,* 216-224.

Back, K. W., & Taylor, R. C. Self-help groups: Tool or symbol? *Journal of Applied Behavioral Sciences,* 1976, *12*(3), 295-309.

Bailey, R. *Radicals in urban politics: The Alinsky approach.* Chicago: University of Chicago Press, 1974.

Lind, A. The future of citizen involvement. *The Futurist,* 1975, *9*(6), 316-320, 323-328.

Marburger, C. Cited in C. S. Mott Foundation, *For Your Information, 22* (November 30, 1976), 8. Flint, Michigan: C. S. Mott Foundation, 1976.

Porter, C. "Manleyville:" Implementing community education through simulation. *Community Education Journal,* 1974, *4*(3), 13-14.

Shafer, P. A suburban model for citizen involvement. *Community Education Journal,* 1974, 4(6), 40, 45.

The National Self-Help Resource Center. *Community resource centers: The notebook.* Washington D. C.: The National Self-Help Resource Center, 1976.

Warden, J. *Malpractice in community work.* Unpublished paper, University of Virginia, Mid-Atlantic Center for Community Education, 1977.

Warren, R. L. *Truth, love, and social change.* Chicago: Rand, McNally, & Co., 1973.

"It is important when developing leadership training programs in any given community to consider the total community, the effects that training one person or groups of persons can have on others in the community." — *Miller*

Chapter 14

Leadership Training Strategies in Community Education

by

Sidney Lynn Miller

LEADERSHIP TRAINING STRATEGIES IN COMMUNITY EDUCATION

When discussing leadership training in community education, there are numerous factors to consider. Such a topic could include discussion of the development of national strategies for training the trainers, methods of training each individual involved in community education at the local level, and many other ideas. For the purpose of this article, discussion will be focused on strategies for training persons involved with community education in a local community, i.e., community education council members, community education coordinators/directors, etc.

An analysis of some specifics necessary to the planning of training strategies is required. First, it is important to analyze the community to determine what persons and groups of persons are involved in the community education program currently, or who have potential for involvement. Examples of these groups include: Boards of Education, superintendents, local government officials, community council members, teachers, principals, agency leaders, community education coordinators, and so on.

The second step is to determine which of these persons or groups of persons should be provided leadership training, and what area of training is most important to each person and/or group. Obviously the role each person is expected to play in the total picture will have much to do with the training determined to be most appropriate for that individual. It is at this point that the trainer and planner of these training programs must consider the answers to the following questions: What role does the community's sponsoring agency expect of a certain individual or group of persons? What role does the professional community educator feel should be expected of a certain individual or group of persons? If there are differences in the answers to the first two questions, can they be resolved either by changing the attitudes of those persons from the sponsoring agency, or by modifying the preferred approach to training? If these differences cannot be resolved immediately, would it be more appropriate to: a) focus training in the areas of agreement; b) spend that energy working to expand the attitudes of the sponsoring agency administrators; c) continue training as if the situation were ideal; or d) devote training efforts to another community? These are not easy questions to answer, but most definitely they are important to the effectiveness of the training that takes place.

It is important when developing leadership training programs in any given community to consider the total community, the effects that training one person or groups of persons can have on others in the community, and the need for integrating the training so that persons or groups of persons develop awarenesses and skills that complement each other rather than hinder the total community education process. For example, it can cause some difficulty if the community education council is provided training that results in role expectations not agreed upon by the program administrators. However, such difficulties may be overcome if council members are taught skills that would be useful in meeting these expectations and if the program administrators are provided training which results in agreement with the same expectations.

The first and most important training session for any person or group of persons involved with community education deals with the topic: What is community education? Even communities that have had what they label a community education program for several years need this introductory session. A discussion of how the concept evolved, of the various components of a community education program, of what community education has looked like in the particular community with which the session participants are involved, of the various other forms community education has taken nationally, and of the potential outcomes of community education programs will help individuals to gain a complete understanding of the concept. This understanding will prepare the participants for contribution to the concept's development and, most importantly, will provide a sound foundation from which to plan, develop and conduct other training sessions. For example, if an individual understands that community involvement is a major part of the community education process, a training session dealing with the developing and conducting of assessments will be much simpler, since the groundwork has been laid to assist those receiving the training to understand WHY it is advantageous to involve community members in the conducting of the survey and in the determination of the programs to be offered.

The community education council is the key to the lasting success of a community education program. Certainly, there must be backing and commitment to the concept's implementation by a sponsoring agency, most frequently the Board of Education. However, once this commitment has been made, the members of the community must carry it through. It is often thought that the community education coordinator/director is the person most important to the community education program. The coordinator/director is important, but the author suggests that the lasting effectiveness of any community education program is only as strong as its community members and community council. Superintendents and community education directors may come and go, but the community members themselves will have a certain amount of stability. Furthermore, the potential for accomplishment through community education can only begin to be met when the community members themselves are involved in the concept's growth.

Once the solid base for training has been laid, or in other words, once there is an understanding of the community education concept among the various community members, the focus of training should be directed toward the community education council and the community education coordinator/director. There are several ways to accomplish this. The first way, which appears to be the most practical from the trainer's point of view, is to bring together a number of coordinators/directors and provide training for them. Upon completion of this training, the directors would then be expected to return to their individual community councils and provide the same form of training for these councils. Unfortunately, what often happens is that the coordinators/directors cannot or will not take the time to attend the training sessions, or if they do, may never get to the point of sharing the information and skills learned with their councils. Even in those cases where there is an effort made by the coordinator to share the training, it may not be as effective.

The second way to provide the training is directly to the community council. The local directors will most likely feel that their role demands that they be in attendance during the training session and that such a procedure allows them to be active participants. During these sessions, the coordinator can obtain the same knowledge and skills as the council members, and at the same time get first-hand contact with the ideas of the members of the council as they ask questions of the trainer. Although the training sessions with the community council will cover many topics, and even though the first training session develops an understanding of the community education concept, it is important that the trainer continually weave the philosophy of community education into training presentations. This can be done by stressing how the topic of the training session is important to the success of community education programs and how various skills being learned are important to the fulfillment of community education goals and objectives.

The first training session with the community councils, which develops an understanding of the community education concept, is most appropriately followed by a session that clarifies the role of the individual community council member and the role, responsibility, and structure of the community education council as a whole.

For the second training session, it is recommended that the following persons be in attendance: a) community council members; b) the community education coordinator/director; and c) a representative of the sponsoring agency's administration (the individual serving as the administrator responsible for the community education program). During this session the need for structure, rules, by-laws, policies, and procedures should be discussed. Procedures must be formulated regarding the development of council guidelines and by-laws with examples of the various topics that should be covered, such as membership requirements, officers, roles and responsibilities, authority, group procedure. By the end of this session there should be commitment to the development of council guidelines, a means outlined for so doing, and a completion date determined.

The exciting thing about doing a training session on community council structure early in the council's development is that it provides the council with one of its first tasks: the development of the by-laws of the group. It is also a sure way for the council to become involved in the accomplishment of a goal, and, at the same time, provides the council with a framework within which to operate in the future.

Now that the community council is developing some identity, an important learning experience can take place that will affect the majority of the council's endeavors. A training session which teaches group skills, primarily in "How to Run a Council Meeting" and "How to Set an Agenda" is in order. These three areas of training: 1) the community education concept; 2) council by-laws; and 3) group process, should take about three sessions, each about three hours in length. They provide a strong foundation from which the council can continue to grow and accomplish its goals.

Other training sessions should be provided as appropriate, based on the needs of the council members as well as the projects in which they are involved or in which they plan to be involved at some future date. Additional training sessions could realistically cover such topics as: goal setting, community assessments, proposal writing, financing community education programs, and planning and evaluating community education programs.

The development of such skills will provide the community education coordinator/director with extra staff while at the same time allowing the council members to truly be involved in the community education process and program development. Training sessions in the topic areas covered above should not simply be simulation type exercises. If appropriately timed, such training sessions can be learning situations which have as their end product both a new skill and a desired outcome, i.e., a resource assessment, or an evaluation instrument which will be used to evaluate the past and/or future year's progress.

The desired outcome of providing training sessions for community education councils and coordinators/directors include: a) the transference of new knowledge to the participants; b) interaction and discussion among the council members and between the members and coordinators/directors; c) a usuable skill or product; d) the ability of the participants to use their new skills and knowledge to further maintain and expand their program without further assistance from the trainer; and e) the participants' confidence in their ability to stay involved and active as productive members of the community education programs.

Hopefully, the trainer will be available for "refresher" sessions for the participants and new persons who become involved in the program. However, the trainer can help both the council and her/himself by providing written materials and by discussing each step of the training program as the session goes along so that, as time passes, those persons remaining on the council can assist new members in understanding concepts learned during various training sessions.

"Community educators must have some logical and sequential way of processing information to obtain results through people." — *Porter*

Chapter 15

Resource Management and Allocation Strategies for the Community Educator

by

Charles F. Porter

RESOURCE MANAGEMENT AND ALLOCATION STRATEGIES FOR THE COMMUNITY EDUCATOR

The Director of Community Education is a person who needs both program and process skills. As an administrator he or she has both a leadership and a managerial function. While community educators readily think of themselves as leaders, administrators, and even facilitators, they seldom think of themselves as managers. According to one management definition adopted by General Electric, managerial work was defined as planning, organizing, integrating, and measuring. Management, then, is basically a problem solving approach that gets things done through others. David Emery (1970) feels that a manager is an information processor and a communicator.

It is this writer's contention that information of any kind can be considered a resource that can be used to solve problems. In order to assist others in solving community problems, community educators must have some logical and sequential way of processing information to obtain results through people. Emery (1970) has come up with five categories that represent all kinds of information with which managers must deal. These categories of information are very applicable to the managing role of the community educator. They are illustrated in the following schema:

CONTINUOUS CYCLE OF INFORMATION-PROCESSING

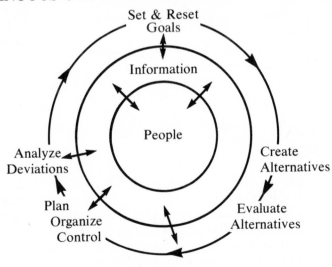

Figure 15-1

First of all information comes from the people in the community. The community educator should formulate some kind of process of information gathering that assists the community (advisory council) in deciding where they are, where they want to go, and how they want to shape the development of their community education philosophy. Once the community knows where it wants to go, then goals should be prioritized, alternative approaches created and evaluated. The best alternative is then selected, and the planning, organizing, and controlling phase of information-processing is implemented. This is followed by analysis of deviations and the shaping of new goals or the reshaping of old ones.

This management of resources information processing is a continuous cycle and should result in a continuous upgrading of community education goals with new and better alternatives. The core of this management cycle is the interaction between people and information.

While all five steps of this management information process cycle are important, the writer would like to elaborate more on the fourth step, namely planning, organizing, and controlling.

Planning

Many community educators spend much of their time reacting to events rather than planning. While there is a need for both short and long term planning, what is really needed is continous planning.

The planning process involves the following:

1. translating broad goals into measurable objectives establishing priorities;
2. identifying what must be done to get desired results;
3. allocating human and material resources;
4. specifying when each activity must occur; and
5. evaluating progress at scheduled check points.

Obviously, a plan is basically a schedule of activities.

Resource management implies planning. For a community educator who sees his/her job as assisting in bringing community resources to bear on community problems, there is evidence that a system approach to planning can be of great help. A systematic method in community education means a step-by-step approach in which the sequence and content of each step has been determined by the relationship of that step to the activities as a whole. Over the years of implementation community educators have focused their attention on key elements in the process and on the critical relationship that must exist between elements in order to be successful.

Management Tools for Community Education

Several management strategies used in business management (Candoli, *et al.,* 1973) are especially appropriate for utilization in community education settings.

1. *Network Analysis* is a managerial technique which is useful in system design, planning, and control. There are two networks that may be useful to community educators: CPM and PERT.

   a. *CPM - Critical Path Method* is determination of the minimum time needed to complete a series of crucial events in any project from start to finish, such as conducting a needs assessment.

ILLUSTRATION OF CRITICAL PATH FOR PROJECT COMPLETION

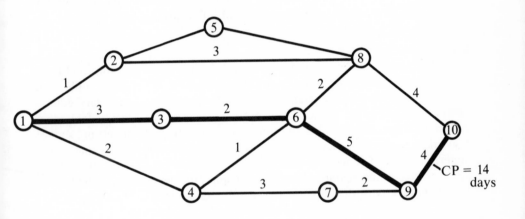

Figure 15-2

If there were ten events in the process of conducting a needs assessment, the critical path would be the longest way through the network. (See Figure 15-2.) In this case, the critical path is the heavy line including events 1, 3, 6, 9, and 10. The events, which take 14 days, are critical to meeting the completion time, because all other paths take fewer days, which leaves slack time available. The critical path has the maximum time involved. The fourteen days is the absolute minimum needed to complete the task with no slack time available, and so this route is the critical path in the network.

b. *PERT - Program Evaluation Review Technique* is also based on critical path scheduling. The fundamental difference is that PERT is applicable where there is no established system for doing the task and therefore, no exact basis for estimating the required time to complete each task. An example would be any new or unique program. CPM scheduling is used on traditional activities or jobs that have been done before, such as community surveys. PERT and CPM have been found to be useful in the internal management of projects, the reporting of progress on a consistent basis to the funding agency, and as the evaluation tool for proposed projects.

2. *GANTT Charts* is a tool used by education managers to give themselves and others a clear visual picture of the calendar of events in a project. It is a simple time-based objective and activities chart, not probabilistic in nature. It is a helpful device when outside activities have to unexpectedly be scheduled into a project.

Organizing

The purpose of organizing is to establish the formal and informal relationships between people and activities that must efficiently implement plans. The purposes of Porter's (1973) "Manleyville," community education simulation game for advisory councils, is to give them a feel for a community education implementation process in a three-hour setting, so that they may understand their relationship to the process as well as that of the superintendent of schools or of the director of community education. They see their role in the development of philosophy, the needs survey, the formulation of objectives, the implementation process, and the evaluation process.

In organizing a community education effort the director must watch for confusion over who is responsible (the council or the director), jealousy over authority, lack of cooperation, communication breakdowns, and excessive demands on his/her time.

Time as a Resource

The most important resource to which a director has access and over which he/she has possible control is his or her time. According to the Northwest Community Education Center (1974), coordinators should analyze how they spend their time in various administrative, supervisory, operational, and facilitative tasks. Prioritization of these tasks according to those which are of high importance, and of crucial importance, and elimination of the others that are time wasters, or of low priority, are excellent methods for better allocation of time.

176

Good managers learn to delegate responsibility in order to use their time more wisely. Some guidelines for managing time wisely are:

1. organize one's work environment;
2. organize one's desk work;
3. be organized and selective when using the telephone;
4. learn to say no; and
5. learn to delegate.

Controlling

Controlling means keeping things on track. Emery (1970) states that a good tracking system should be sensitive, analytical, diplomatic, corrective, and economical. One can use a centrally controlled system or a decentralized one. Trust is probably best developed in a decentralized approach and seems more appropriate for the practitioner of the philosophy of community education.

Management by Objectives

MBO could be one useful tool in the control process of community education management, especially in large school districts. Increased delegation of responsibility and multiple levels of accountability are needed where complexity of operations are on the increase. MBO is a system which enables an organization to plan in advance through commonly accepted goals by all involved. The specific objectives that are created together by the total group fosters genuine communication. MBO focuses on evaluative achievement of employees' goals, and enhances commitment to these goals. MBO focuses on results, not personalities.

SUMMARY

The mission of community education is to serve people through better utilization of all community resources. The community educator not only needs the knowledge of social systems and human behavior, but must also begin to develop the technical skills needed for organizational management. He or she not only needs the process skills of coordinating, surveying, demonstrating, programming, training, and promoting as identified by Weaver (1972), but the director must also have the management skills of planning, organizing, staffing, directing, and controlling the organization to which he or she belongs.

REFERENCES

Candoli, I. C., Hack, W. G., Ray, J. R., & Stollar, D. H. *School business administration: A planning approach.* Boston: Allyn & Bacon, Inc., 1973.

Emery, D. A. *The compleat manager.* New York: McGraw-Hill Book Co., 1970.

Northwest Community Education Development Center. *Time management for community school coordinators.* Eugene, Oregon: University of Oregon, 1974.

Porter, C. F. *Manleyville: Community education simulation game.* Fort Collins, Colorado: Colorado State University, 1973.

Weaver, D. C. *The emerging community education model.* Kalamazoo, Michigan: Western Michigan University, 1972.

"Taking away some of the pressure to produce quick results may in the long run free the community educator to do a better job in the development of a continued process of needs assessment." — *Jeffrey*

Chapter 16

Processing as A Community Education Strategy

by

John B. Jeffrey

PROCESSING AS A COMMUNITY EDUCATION STRATEGY

Assume for a moment that you have just been hired as community education director in Anyville, U.S.A. Assume further that Anyville has never before had a community education program and that it is your task to develop such a program. How will you begin your task? How will you determine areas of need in the community? How will you find resources to meet these needs? How will you get to know community members and gain their acceptance and trust? In short, how will you "process for community education?"

Certainly your responses to these questions would depend upon many factors. Perhaps the most important factor would be the amount of background work done prior to your arrival. If you have been hired by the superintendent and curtly told to "start a community education program," your task is formidable. On the other hand, your task will be a great deal easier if a competent community task force has studied the concept, visited communities with operative programs, reported enthusiastically to the Board of Education, generated a broad base of support among key community residents, and developed a comprehensive position description. Most likely, your position in Anyville falls somewhere between the two extremes outlined above; i.e., there is limited community support and understanding of the concept and you have some idea of what is expected of you. The paragraphs which follow will assume this "middle position" and provide an outline of steps to be taken in "processing for community education."

Whitt (1971), writing about all school officials, provided a clue to the most important initial task for the new director:

> School personnel have to stop thinking in terms of here is the school and there is the community. The school staff has to go out into the community and get to know it and the only way the school system can reach out is for the people in the school to leave the hallowed halls of academic learning and visit with the people who live in the community, who pay their salaries, and who provide them the raw materials for their livelihood . . . Essentially, what must happen is for schools to develop good human relations rather than good public relations. (pp. 17-18)

Stated simply, the most important beginning task for the new community education director is to get to know the community. The most effective way to begin this task is to simply get out into the community and knock on doors. The director can present his business card, introduce himself, and identify himself with a "new program at the school." A willingness to knock on doors and REALLY listen will provide tangible results.

The author's own experience at introducing community education in the method described above produced the following results: some initial program needs were discovered; several complaints about the school system were heard; a few potential community council members were identified; several community needs were identified; one elderly resident indicated that he had lived in the district for 33 years and that no one from the schools had ever come to his home before; and several barking dogs were encountered without injury to the new director.

In addition to speaking with community residents as individuals, the new director can make presentations to various community groups. Social, service, school, civic, and religious groups are usually most willing to permit the community educator to make a presentation at one of their meetings. This initial presentation to a community group might include the screening of a film about the concept (*"To Touch A Child," "A Sense of Community,"* etc.), followed by a discussion of how the concept might apply to the local community. An important rule of thumb for the new director during these discussions is the admonition that God gave the community education directors "two ears and only one mouth so that he or she would listen twice as much as talk."

Presentations to community groups offer several advantages to the new director. First, they provide an opportunity to present information about the concept in a non-threatening manner. Second, they offer community group members an opportunity to ask questions about the concept and to provide input into how the concept might function in their community. Third, they provide evidence that the new director is a school official who is willing to leave the school building and get out into the community in an effort to work with community residents in the identification and solution of local problems. Finally, visits with local groups enable the community educator to begin to establish an important bank of community resources. It is difficult to overestimate the importance of the benefits outlined above.

In addition to meeting with community residents and organized groups, the director must soon begin the rather formidable task of gathering hard data about the structure and makeup of the community. Although no two communities are exactly alike, it is suggested that the community educator in any community should be familiar with:

1. The history of the community - this would include information about the beginning of the community and its development. Of particular importance would be knowledge of the kinds of people who settled the area and the major influences which have affected growth.
2. Governmental organization - many communities are fractional parts of many different political units. Of particular relevance here would

be the knowledge of how the school relates to these governments both financially and politically.
3. Business and industry - major business and industrial developments should be noted with special attention to their economic contribution to the community.
4. Religion - kinds and numbers of denominations and sects which represent the various segments of the population should be identified.
5. Education - not only would it be necessary to know about the public school system and the area it covers but other educational operations should be identified as well.
6. Agencies - social agencies such as United Fund, government-supported agencies such as the employment security commission, welfare, health, and recreation.
7. Communication systems - it would be necessary to know all the media sources, such as radio, television, newspapers, and other community publications. (Minzey & LeTarte, 1972, pp. 54-55)

It is important to note, lest one become too discouraged, that much of the above information has already been collected by other people and groups. Sources of such information include census statistics; data collected by bicentennial study groups; information shelved at the local library; data (often very sophisticated) which has been collected by local industry and public utilities; results of studies conducted by other community groups; and information filed in the minds of the local senior citizenry. The community educator, to save time and avoid the pitfalls of a second "discovery of the wheel," is advised to make full use of such data.

The next step in "processing for community education" in Anyville is the establishment of some highly visible program offerings. Many fervent advocates of needs assessment would hold that this should not be done without a formal determination of community needs. At this point in the development of the community education process, however, a formal needs assessment is neither warranted nor necessary. The purpose of these initial program offerings is to get school lights on, bring people into the buildings, and meet the expectations of school board members and community residents who want to see highly visible programs activities. Several widely popular class offerings (cake decorating, volleyball, and sewing with stretch materials) will suffice to accomplish these purposes.

The above comments should not be construed to mean that needs assessment is not an important part of the community education concept. To the contrary, it is a highly important and integral part of the concept. However, the notion that it is a sin to offer a few widely-accepted programs without a formal needs assessment is naive. In fact, the above process, by taking away some of the pressure to produce quick results, may in the long run free the community educator to do a better job in the development of a continued process of needs assessment. This idea will be addressed later in this chapter.

At this point in the development of community education in Anyville, the director has accomplished several important objectives. He or she has ventured into the community to meet individuals and groups, collected and studied hard data about the community, and brought people into lighted school facilities by offering several popular program activities. Unfortunately, many "Anyvilles" never move very far beyond this state in their development. They offer more and more programs and count more and more participants, yet they fail to move into the critical area of COMMUNITY INVOLVEMENT. One way to avoid this pitfall is through the development of advisory councils.

Large communities often organize community advisory councils at each elementary school while smaller communities many times form one council to serve the entire district. Regardless of which organizational pattern that is selected, well functioning councils provide the catalyst which makes for REAL community education:

> People are not to be involved in advisory councils just for involvement sake. Their participation in assessing needs, planning programs, and evaluating progress actually does produce better decisions. And better decisions result in better educational programs. The democratic principle? Yes. Belief in this principle is based upon the long-tested knowledge that the people, given the essential facts and freedom to express their views, will make the best decisions in matters that affect their own welfare. (Parson & Seay, 1974, p. 171)

The author's experience indicates that four factors are crucial to the success of advisory councils. First, advisory council membership must be broadly reflective of the makeup of the community as a whole. The system for selecting members, whether appointive or elective, must have provisions which insure representation beyond active, vocal citizens who tend to dominate community groups. Second, the council must provide for effective two-way communication with the community as a whole. Often, community concerns are voiced to the council without corresponding feedback regarding council action (or lack of action) related to the concern. Third, the council must develop its own unique method of identifying community problems, finding appropriate resources to attack these problems, and developing the momentum necessary to begin the problem solving process. Finally, and perhaps most important, the council must experience some successes during the first few months of its existence. Success breeds enthusiasm and enthusiasm provides opportunity for more success.

The reader will note that little in the way of specific suggestions regarding council operations has been offered. It is the author's contention that the methodology of needs identification, resource allocation, and problem solving should come from within the council itself. Obviously, the expertise of the director will be helpful as these decisions are made, but he or she is advised to be wary of what Warden (1974) has referred to as engineered consent of citizens in ritualistic council settings. In short, the director should beware that council activities are truly reflective of community desires and not "rubber-stamps" of the director's ideas.

A related step in "processing for community education" is the development of a methodology for increased cooperation and communication among local agencies. Often, a major problem in the community is not a lack of resources but rather a lack of coordination of these resources. An agency roundtable (council), meeting on a bi-weekly or monthly basis, can serve to increase communications among agency groups. The community education director, serving as the catalyst for the establishment of the roundtable, enhances his or her esteem in the community as he or she is increasingly viewed as one who unselfishly brings people together in service to the entire community.

Once "personal agendas" and fears have been discussed, the agency roundtable serves several functions. The increased communication mentioned above provides agency personnel with an awareness of the roles and functions of other agencies in the community. It is amazing and somewhat frightening that agencies know so little about one another. Further, increased communication provides for the enhancement of vital trust relationships among these groups. In addition, agencies become aware of how they can tap one another's resources, avoid duplication of services, and "team-up" to develop the synergy needed to tackle difficult community problems. Finally, and increasingly more important, the agency roundtable provides a forum for the development of joint funding proposals.

Attention is now directed to a concept alluded to earlier — formal needs assessment. Community educators often confuse needs assessment with an annual check-list survey mailed to community residents. At best these surveys provide some limited information about the kinds of programs which interest a limited segment of the target population. At worst they are a waste of time and effort because they fail to uncover real community needs. Allan (1974) has indicated that results of these surveys are suspect because the information garnered is not representative of the entire community: the people who return the surveys might represent biased groups within the community; returns may note superficial WANTS but seldom real NEEDS of people; and returns are likely to be disproportionate, resulting in programming which does not accurately reflect the desires of the community as a whole.

Real community needs assessment is part of a continual process of which a community needs questionnaire is only a small part. Much of this process has already been outlined above. In fact, the new director has begun the process of needs assessment when he or she knocks on the first door during the first community visit. In addition, a great deal of valuable information is gathered through coffee-shop conversation, meetings with community residents following a session of the P.T.O., informal chats in the "downtown area," conversations with individuals involved in initial program offerings, contacts with local service groups, attendance at senior-citizen meetings, dialogues with clergy, etc. These contacts provide for the development of a trust relationship with community residents — a vital initial step in the needs assessment process.

The director who has done a good job of collecting and digesting hard data about the structure and makeup of the community has begun a second step in this process. Data collected probably document a myriad of community problems and needs. In addition, these data often point to resources available to aid in the solution of these problems.

Council groups constitute a third, and extremely vital, step in assessing community needs. There is simply no substitute for this communication link with the entire community. This link provides detailed information regarding community needs and offers an invaluable opportunity to send information back to community residents.

Council groups and the agency roundtable groups should be deeply involved in a fourth step in the needs assessment process — the needs assessment instrument. There is a world of difference between a check-list survey designed by the community education director and a needs assessment instrument DESIGNED, DISTRIBUTED, COLLECTED, and ANALYZED by council people. They put the COMMUNITY into the community needs instrument. Full advisory council involvement helps insure the development of an instrument which collects data desired by community residents rather than just by the director. Most important, council involvement in the collection and analysis of the data makes it easier to further involve members in working at solutions to identified problems.

Hopefully, the steps outlined above have provided a generous list of Anyville's needs (programmatic and otherwise). At this point in the development of community education in Anyville, the new director and the advisory council will prioritize these needs in an effort to determine which need will receive initial action. When this has been accomplished, the council will mobilize and allocate resources which they believe can best meet the identified target needs. REAL community education is now happening in Anyville!

Space has not permitted the author to deal with several other issues germane to the development of community education in Anyville (e.g., budgeting, programming, evaluation, etc.). However, it is hoped that the information provided has given the reader some idea of the steps involved in "processing for community education." Certainly, there is no one "sure fire" method of organizing the process. However, some of the basics have been outlined here in the hope that they stimulate the reader's thought processes.

One final thought: organizing Anyville for the process is a difficult undertaking. It cannot be done alone. The new director is urged to contemplate the ancient wisdom of Lao Tse (525 B.C.):

A leader is best
When people barely know he exists.
Not so good when people obey and acclaim him.
Worse when they despise him.
"Fail to honour people"
"They fail to honour you"
But of a good leader who talks little,
When his work is done, his aim fulfilled,
They will say, "We did this ourselves." (Allan, 1974, p. 9)

REFERENCES

Allan, D. *Assessing community needs — a primer.* Pamphlet produced by Center for Community Education, Eastern Michigan University, Ypsilanti, Mich., 1974.

Minzey, J. D., & LeTarte, C. E. *Community education: From program to process.* Midland, Mich.: Pendell Publishing, 1972.

Parson, S. R., & Seay, M. F. Advisory councils in community education. In M. F. Seay & Associates, *Community education: A developing concept.* Midland, Michigan: Pendell Publishing Co., 1974.

Warden, J. W. *How community is community education?* Pamphlet produced by Center for Community Education, Eastern Michigan University, Ypsilanti, Mich., 1974.

Whitt, R. L. *A handbook for the community school director.* Midland, Mich.: Pendell Publishing, 1971.

"Organization Development as a function is, in a way, both a response (or reaction) to the increasingly rapid rate of change as well as a vehicle for proactively and deliberately causing change to occur." — Ault

Chapter 17

Organization Development Strategies Applied to Community Education

by

Dick Ault

ORGANIZATION DEVELOPMENT STRATEGIES APPLIED TO COMMUNITY EDUCATION

It is the intent of this paper to address those practitioners in the field of community education who are in a position for and have an interest in bringing about change in the systems of which they are a part but who may not be too familiar with the concepts of Organization Development. These potential change agents may wear a variety of hats and go under sundry titles (e.g., Community School Director, Superintendent, Principal, Teacher-Consultant, etc.). What they will find in this chapter is an introductory overview of an approach to planned change called Organization Development or OD, with some focus of that overview on the field of community education. They will also find some of the citations obviously refer to industrial organizations but the transfer to community education should not be difficult.

Although OD formally originated in industry (French, 1972), leaders in education have long contributed to the field (see, for example, Bennis *et al.,* 1969; Havelock, 1970; Schmuck, 1971). According to French (1972), the behavioral science underpinnings of OD generally emerge from three mainstreams of social science research and activity: "(1) the laboratory training movement; (2) survey research and feedback methodology; and, basic to both of these, (3) the writings, efforts, energy, and impetus of the late Kurt Lewin" (p. 1). A fourth stream would be added by many — the open systems stream with its roots in general systems theory but brought to organization theory by people such as Katz and Kahn (1966), Emery and Trist (1965) and others.

No entirely satisfactory definition of OD exists, but among the most widely used is Beckhard's (1969) which, in effect, defines OD as a planned process for increasing organization effectiveness and health through interventions based on behavioral science knowledge. If the phrase "and/or community" is added after "organization," a definition results that could encompass community education. The remainder of this paper will break that definition down and examine its key parts, especially as they apply to community education.

PLANNED

The concept of *planned* change is key. Much change occurs. It has become trite to say this is an era of increasingly rapid change. According to Bennis (1969), "Change is the biggest story in the world today and it is affecting all institutions — corporations, unions, communities, governments, schools and universities, societies and even the international order

. . . (and) we are not coping with it adequately" (p. 1). In other words, while change is certainly occurring in or to all of our social systems, much of it is not planned. Much social system change is reactive to outside pressure. School systems, of course, are not immune to this. They need change just to keep up, as Peets (1970) stated, quoting Pelligrin's phrase regarding "being buffeted about by the pressures and demands of society" as opposed to engaging in "planned change" (p. 18).

OD as a function is, in a way, both a response (or reaction) to the increasingly rapid rate of change as well as a vehicle for proactively and deliberately causing change to occur. It is "widely used as a modality for producing change" (Nielson, 1977, p. 407), while at the same time "is a response to change, a complex educational strategy intended to change the beliefs, attitudes, values, and structures of organizations (and/or communities) so that they can better adapt to new technologies, markets, and challenges, and the dizzying rate of change itself" (Bennis, 1969, p. 2).

A philosophical question for community educators, in this regard, is whether community education should be seen as purely a service to meet the expressed needs of school and school community or as a force for change in shaping the community. Certainly its origins in depression era Flint were a combination of both aims and perhaps in that integration lies the answer.

A PROCESS

OD, it is often said, should not be viewed as a *program* — programs typically being viewed as having a definitive beginning and end — but as a process, a closed-loop process that is never ending. In fact, it is often said that OD must, if it is to be successful, become "a way of life." The process is variously described but the model in Figure 17-1 by Frohman and Kolb (Kolb *et al.,* 1971, p. 355) is a fair representation of a consensus. Frohman and Kolb (Kolb *et al.,* 1971) suggest that the change agent's critical task during the scouting phase is to determine appropriate entry points into the system, focusing on understanding both the formal and informal power structure. This notion is supported by the adoption/diffusion literature regarding the critical role of opinion leaders in bringing about change. (See, e.g., Rogers, 1962.) Kolb *et al.* (1971) cautioned, this is "particularly important in . . . attempts to introduce change in systems where the power structure and human interrelationships are ambiguous or diffuse. In community development, for example, it is crucial" (p. 356).

THE PROCESS OF PLANNED CHANGE

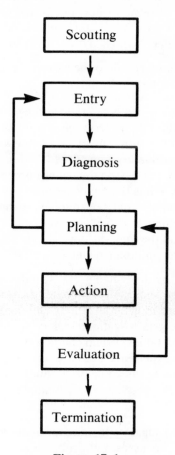

Figure 17-1

In addition to power, other writers emphasize the need in scouting to determine the "readiness" of the system for change (Beckhard, 1969 and 1975; Glidewell, 1959). This sensing includes the search for the "felt needs" of the system.

The best opportunities occur when problems exist for which there is no "standard" procedural or bureaucratic solution, and where the managers involved are really bothered by their difficulty in coping. Look for these problems where new technology is being introduced (e.g., computers); where a problem required close collaboration and coordination across functional lines (e.g., "business areas"); where organizational boundaries are being changed (e.g., mergers and takeovers); where organization restructuring of any kind is taking place; where physical locations are being changed or new plants and facilities being built and commissioned; or where the organization is expanding or contracting rapidly (e.g., redundancies). (Harrison, 1971, p. 1)

(The community counterparts to the above "problems" or "opportunities" would seem apparent.)

In addition to opinion leaders, other strategic system members may need to be discovered during this scouting phase. Rogers (1962) also refers to "gate-keepers" as quite a different species. Gate-keepers may or may not lead opinion, but as legitimately constituted authorities within the formal system, they are in positions to stop the change process or allow it to occur, to shut or open the gate. While they may not need to be involved to the same extent as opinion leaders, they must be involved to the extent that they are at least "neutralized" so that they will not stop the effort. Harrison (1971) further suggests being on the look-out for "the forces in the (system) which are supportive of change and improvement" (p. 1).

This is supported by Rothman's (1974) exhaustive review of recent research in social change, especially community change. He wraps the findings together into important generalizations and corollary action guidelines for practitioners. These generalizations include finding high innovativeness positively related to such target system characteristics as "a modern orientation" (p. 424), positive experience (and absence of previous negative experience) with innovations, felt need or discontentment, and supportive value orientations including "liberalism, scientism and nonauthoritarianism" (p. 435).

Harrison (1971) also suggests looking for multiple entry points: "a variety of people, groups, processes and problems with which contact can be made and to which help may be given" (p. 1). In searching for these entry points, the consultant is advised by Harrison (1971, p. 2) to look for promising arenas, "relatively healthy parts of the system . . . with individuals and groups which have as much freedom and discretion in managing their own operations as possible" (Harrison, 1971, p. 2).

The general readiness question in scouting is neatly summed up in a formula by Gleicher: "C = (abd) > x, where C = change, a = level of dissatisfaction with the status quo, b = clear or understood desired state, d = knowledge of entry strategies, and x = 'cost' of changing" (Beckhard, 1975, p. 45). The combination, in other words, of felt need, the clarity of a goal or preferred future, and know-how regarding practical starting points must be greater than the money, time and energy required in changing in order for that change to occur. A practitioner must assess all of this in the scouting period.

Entry points having been chosen, the consultant begins, in the Frohman-Kolb model, the entry process itself with building a contract (or series of contracts) with the client system. This may or may not be a legal document and often exists purely as a "psychological contract." In any case, it defines mutual expectations regarding how future stages in the change process will be carried out (Kolb, p. 356). While given here as an early entry issue, the dynamic nature of change calls for keeping the contract open for continual renegotiation.

Perhaps one of the clearest cases of effective scouting and entry is the most classic story in the annals of community education, the pursuit of Charles Stewart Mott by Frank Manley, Sr. Manley was obviously the change agent. The community was Flint. Manley wanted to use the schools for recreation programs ("to give every boy a bat and ball") to reduce or prevent juvenile delinquency (a felt need). He attempted to sell this idea to community group after group after group. Finally, he found an interested party: Charles Stewart Mott. Mott wanted Boys' Clubs and was also known to be chary with a dollar (two felt needs). This author has been in the audience when Manley told this story and heard him say, "I had been hunting with a shotgun; after finding Mr. Mott, I switched to a rifle." This statement is consistent with adoption of innovation research by Havelock (1971) who outlined a four-state process of adoption: (1) Awareness; (2) Knowledge; (3) Trial; and (4) Adoption. Stages 1 and 2 are most efficiently accomplished through mass media approaches (hunting with a shotgun) while trial (the first six schools) and adoption (the Flint Community School Program) are best accomplished through personal contact with opinion leaders (switching to a rifle). Note further that, while Manley's goal was reduction of juvenile delinquency, he did not start by focusing on a juvenile delinquent, or for that matter, any of those suffering most in those depression years. That was not, of course, because he was not concerned with them, but rather because it is often (if not usually) futile to go first to the powerless to attempt to bring about change.

However, Manley did also violate one of the principles of entry suggested above, that of finding "multiple entry points." He admitted in later years that his single-minded idea that sports would be the answer for everyone had been based on his own life's experience and that he had subsequently learned that other people and other problems might be more suitably addressed by "entry points" other than a bat and ball.

Having analyzed the entry, it is important to review a most critically important phase: diagnosis. Dalton described this step as essentially a job of drawing conclusions from an intensive diagnosis of the situation. If an analysis is to be more than an academic exercise, it must reach decisions about: (a) What are the specific problems to be corrected? (b) What are the determinants of these problems? and (c) What forces are likely to work for and against change? Answers to these questions are difficult to derive because managers are easily overinvolved or insulated from the sources of problems in their organizations. A variety of diagnostic techniques may have to be employed — such as the use of meetings, consultants, conferences, task forces, interviews, questionnaire surveys, informal conversations, and so forth. The central concern here is to gather reasonably *valid* information that is not skewed to fit only the biases of a few managers or a newly hired outside consultant. Because the impact of organization change can be so significant, we believe it pays to spend sufficient time in this stage to gather information from a wide range of sources and to accomplish this through a variety of data-gathering techniques. (p. 2)

Planning proceeds from the diagnosis. This diagnosis may turn up data that give rise to the need for "a renegotiation of the entry contract" (Kolb, p. 357), and thus the return arrow from planning back to entry in the Frohman-Kolb model in Figure 17-1. Planning includes objectives to be achieved (thus working on variable b in the Gleicher formula) and solutions or strategies to be tried (thus working on variable d).

Action has already taken place, of course. Some one or more people have already done something to, with, or in the system during scouting, entry, diagnosis and planning. However, the action phase of the model refers more specifically here to the system's actions to implement those solutions or strategies determined in the planning phase.

Some solutions or strategies may work and some may not. It is necessary to evaluate to know which is the case. This evaluation may involve archival data, surveys, critical incidents or many other techniques. It is often a difficult phase of OD to accomplish, especially the "human systems" aspect of an OD intervention. As Jones (1975) says, "The things that can be measured precisely are relatively unimportant in human relations" (p. 117). Nevertheless, it is important. Evaluation is, in a sense, a rediagnosis of the system or a diagnosis of the system in a new state, and thus, the feedback arrow to planning in the model shown. This looping phenomenon causes the OD approach to be seen as an on-going process rather than as a program with a beginning and an end.

While the process goes on, the consultant or change agent's work with the system may end — thus, the "Termination" phase. It has long been stated as a rule of thumb in OD that the consultant's goal is to work himself or herself out of a job. This requires building internal capacity in the client system for sustaining the process. This requirement leads to the inclusion in some models of a phase called "institutionalization."

A general concept in OD is that it is and should be a transactional and collaborative process (Bennis, *et al.*, 1969). Hence, the change agent and the client system would engage jointly in all stages shown in the Frohman-Kolb model.

INTERVENTIONS BASED ON BEHAVIORAL SCIENCE KNOWLEDGE

The underlying roots of behavioral science knowledge from which OD grows were referred to at the beginning of this paper. Interventions based on this tradition are many and varied, but perhaps can be summarized into clusters or "families" of tools such as the following (French, 1973): diagnostic techniques; survey-feedback-action planning; team building; intergroup techniques (and conflict management generally); work design; goal-setting and planning; education and training; and open systems approaches. There is not space here in this overview to go into detail on these interventions. French and Bell (1973) provide an excellent introduction to these families of tools. All of them, however, would seem to have an appropriateness to community education.

SUMMARY

This paper attempted an overview of an approach to planned change known as Organization Development (OD) as it applies to community education. Emphasis was put on the planned or "proactive" nature of this approach to change in social systems as opposed to more frequently encountered "reactive" approaches. An introduction to the process of OD was given with a view toward its appropriateness for potential change agents in the field of community education.

It seems clear that there is much from this action-oriented, applied behavioral science discipline that can be used by community educators.

REFERENCES

Beckhard, R. *Organization development: Strategies and models.* Reading, Mass.: Addison-Wesley, 1969.
Beckhard, R. Strategies for large system change. *Sloan Management Review*, 1975, *Winter,* 43-55.

Bennis, W. G. *Organization development: Its nature, origins, and prospects.* Reading, Mass.: Addison-Wesley, 1969.

Bennis, W. G., Benne, K. D., & Chin, R. *The planning of change* (2nd Ed.). New York: Holt, Rinehart and Winston, 1969.

Dalton, G. W., Lawrence, P. R. (Eds.) with Greiner, L. E. *Organization change and development.* Homewood, Ill.: Irwin-Dorsey Press, 1970.

Emery, F., & Trist, E. L. The casual texture of organization environments. *Human Relations,* 1965, *18,* 21-31.

French, W., & Bell, C. A brief history of organization development. *Journal of Contemporary Business,* 1972, *3,* 1-8.

French, W., & Bell, C. *Organization development: Behavioral science interventions for organization improvement.* Englewood Cliffs: Prentice Hall, 1973.

Glidewell, J. C. The entry problem in consultation. *The Journal of Social Issues, 1959, 2,* 51-59.

Harrison, R. Strategy guidelines for an internal organization development unit. *OD Practitioner,* 1971, *3,* 1-4.

Havelock, R. G. *A guide to innovation in education.* Ann Arbor, Mich.: The University of Michigan, 1970.

Havelock, R. G. *Planning for innovation through dissemination and utilization of knowledge.* Ann Arbor, Mich.: The University of Michigan, 1971.

Jones, J. E. Humanistic numbers. In *The 1975 annual handbook for group facilitators.* LaJolla, Calif.: University Associates, 1975.

Katz, D., & Kahn, R. L. *The social psychology of organizations.* New York: Wiley, 1966.

Kolb, D. A., Rubin, I. M., & McIntyre, J. M. *Organizational psychology: An experiential approach.* Englewood Cliffs: Prentice Hall, 1971.

Nielson, W. R. Overview of organization development assessment: Theory, research, and applications. In *Proceedings of the 20th annual conference,* Midwest Division of the Academy of Management, 1977.

Peets, E. F. A comparative study of factors related to innovation in selected public school districts of southern lower Michigan (Doctoral dissertation, Western Michigan University, 1970). *Dissertation Abstracts International,* 1970, *31,* 2073A-2074A. (University Microfilms No. 70-20,138)

Rothman, J. *Planning and organizing for social change.* New York: Columbia University Press, 1974.

Rogers, E. M. *Diffusion of innovations.* New York: The Free Press of Glencoe, 1962.

Schmuck, R. A., & Miles, M. B. *Organization development in schools.* Palo Alto, Calif.: National Press Books, 1971.

"A significant factor in the effectiveness of citizen participation is the existence of different assumptions, values, and concepts regarding citizen participation policy that are held by various lay groups and professional educators in the community." — Nance and Dixon

Chapter 18

Community Education and Third Party Intervention in Educational Decision-Making

by
Everette E. Nance
and
James D. Dixon, II

COMMUNITY EDUCATION AND THIRD PARTY INTERVENTION IN EDUCATIONAL DECISION-MAKING

INTRODUCTION

The philosophy and practice of community education has undergone many changes and much development since its inception. Some of the most recent of these developments seem to center on the involvement of the community and the utilization of community councils. The present discussion will focus on the theoretical underpinnings related to Third Party Intervention Groups in the context of social systems and role theory, and on suggestions for the development of intervention groups as part of the development of community education. There will be no attempt made to explore in depth the historical development of citizen advisory councils and groups. Rather, this paper will discuss these as a basis for describing an innovative kind of citizen participation mechanism, including a brief discussion of some shortcomings in current practices with citizen advisory groups and of what must be done to insure effective, meaningful, and continuous citizen participation in educational decision-making at the school district level. The process herein discussed is generalizable to the school building and community levels as well.

Traditionally, schools have been looked upon as sanctuaries of harmony and content, and, as such, have been recipients of unanimous public adulation, respect, and in some instances, awe. The purposes of such myths have been served admirably. However, they have been increasingly difficult to maintain over longer and longer periods of time. Often the local school and school system are the loci of serious, even potentially explosive, community conflicts. Schools have frequently become targets of increasing public distrust and the objects of diminishing financial and moral support. Political struggles for control, conflict, distrust, and withdrawal of support are pervasive both in breadth and depth, and can be attributed to a variety of factors. The issue of school desegregation is quite often a serious, emotion laden, potentially explosive conflict of community expectations and individual values, as seen in various court cases. Such conflicting points of view often are the root cause for the failure of so-called "innovative" citizen participation enterprises. Fantini (1968) has observed that schools and public education must bear some share of the blame for current crises in contemporary American society.

To counteract such tendencies and shortcomings, the federal government and private foundations have sponsored programs that established school-community agents, parent-teacher associations, and parent and community advisory councils. These were aimed at promoting home, school, and community collaboration and cooperation in resource assessment, utilization, and evaluation (Bayham, 1967). Over the past decade and a half, the federal government alone has spent over a billion dollars on research and development studying the country's pressing educational problems, and billions more on categorical aid to schools and districts. All these programs required some sort of "meaningful" citizen participation. Yet, the problems remain intractable and in a majority of instances the project's citizen participation components that were implemented bore little likeness to the components that were originally conceived. In some instances the citizen participation component did not function at all.

A contributing factor in the success or failure of such projects can be attributed to the orientation of the school district, that is, whether the district followed a "problem solving" orientation or an "opportunistic orientation" toward the use of extramural funds earmarked for citizen participation. Those districts which experienced success in citizen participation enterprises were usually characterized by a strong element of continuous planning and replanning as opposed to a burst of "rushed" planning at the outset. Training of professional staff and citizen participants in successful programs evolved from the on-going needs of the district on a regular basis, and were defined by participants as opposed to that training delivered in "quickie" sessions at the initiation of the project without participant assistance. Also, successful projects insured that all participants, staff and "advisors" had easy access to consistent and committed technical assistance from competent community educators at university centers, state departments of education, and local school district levels. Finally, there was strong affirmative support from key administrators at all levels within the district.

A significant factor in the effectiveness of citizen participation is the existence of different assumptions, values, and concepts regarding citizen participation policy that are held by various lay groups and professional educators in the community. As Getzels (1963) has aptly pointed out, in many citizen participation programs the issue was

> one form or another of conflict — conflict between one position the educator occupies and another, conflict between the educator's needs and the expectations held for him by the patrons of the school's program for citizen involvement, conflict among the values held by the patron groups, those held by the educators themselves, and the institutional values. (p. 309)

Such conflicts are of significance to all three entities because the resolution and/or management of conflict has direct bearing upon the degree and quality of the education in the community. Program planning for citizen participation as a systematic process in the educational setting should provide for conceptual clarification, empirical investigation, and practical management of potential problems. Himes (1968) stated that the principal mechanism by which a highly differentiated society has accomplished tasks which were beyond individual capabilities has been through organization. The development of Third Party Groups working within the broader social system, and particularly when those groups have been associated with schools, has provided a viable organization for optimization of community effectiveness and maximization of community resource utilization. This discussion will now focus on what conceivable roles Third Party Groups can play in the educational decision-making arena within the rubric termed "community education."

THE SCHOOL AS A SOCIAL SYSTEM

It seems that in its most efficacious expression, Third Party Intervention Groups can be vital, dynamic, and broadly effective mechanisms for public school advocacy in general and for human resources development specifically. The neighborhood school, and the school district of which it is a part, are organizations with the broader social system. The term "social system" is a conceptualization used to identify a composite sociological entity. The social systems concept has been defined by Carr (1955) as "an 'assemblage' or aggregation of individuals and institutional locality . . . functioning in various degrees of interdependence as a permanent organized unit of the social order" (p. 166-167).

School organizations as social systems have been defined as hierarchial arrangements or roles which are occupied by individuals functioning to accomplish specific organization purposes and goals. Commenting on Carr's definition, Getzels, Lipham, and Campbell (1968) suggested that "the three charteristics of social systems . . . are the interdependence of parts, their organization into some sort of whole, and the intrinsic presence of both individuals and organizations" (pp. 53-54).

Parsons (June, 1956) identified four types of organizations: (1) those oriented to economic production; (2) those oriented to political goals; (3) those oriented to societal integrative organizations; and (4) those oriented to pattern-maintenance. This last type Parsons (Sept., 1956) defined as "those with primarily cultural, educational, and expressive functions. Perhaps the most clear-cut organizational examples are churches and schools. (Pattern-maintenance is not here conceived to preclude creativity; hence, research is included.)" (pp. 228-229)

Within this categorization the local school may be conceived of as a social sub-system, its administration as a social process, and the general context of administration as a social system. According to Getzels, Lipham, and Campbell (1968), the administration of a school, may be examined from three points of view: structurally, functionally, and operationally. Structurally, it can be seen as "the hierarchy of superordinate-subordinate relationships within a social system." Functionally, the hierarchy of relationships is "the locus for allocating and integrating roles and facilities in order to achieve the goals of the system." Operationally, the administrative process is implemented in "person-to-person interaction" (pp. 53-55).

All three aspects are essential to the effective functioning of the social system. However, the functional point of view is most germane to the present discussion. Third Party Intervention Groups most effectively and efficiently accomplish their goals when their appropriate role and status are defined and elaborated upon in the initial developmental process, and when adequate resources and facilities are provided. The functional viewpoint also provides for the development of procedures, regulation of appropriate task activities, and for both formative and summative evaluation. In further elaboration of the role of organizations, Lipham (1964) suggested that social systems serve to "facilitate the allocation and integration of roles and resources in order to achieve the goals and ends of the system" (pp. 120-121). This function is a significant factor in creating a "climate" for the effective operation of Third Party Intervention Groups. While these bodies function as a part of a particular system — the school district — they also function within the broader social system and have access to a wider range of human and material resources. This factor alone distinguishes the Third Party Intervention Group from the traditional community advisory council.

ROLE THEORY AND CITIZEN PARTICIPATION

Concepts and theoretical formulations related to social systems usually include the term "role." One such concept of role applicable to Third Party Intervention practices was set forth by Getzels and Guba (1957), and includes two dimensions which are significant factors in observing organizational behavior — the personal dimension and the organizational dimension. Each behavioral act of the Third Party Group can be understood in terms of the force by which it is stimulated, based on the interaction of the two dimensions. Thus, "the interactions comprise . . . social behavior" (Getzels and Guba, 1957, p. 423). Role, according to the literature, appears to have three distinct categories of usage: (1) in relation to personality development; (2) in relation to society as a whole; and (3) in relation to specific groups or institutions in a social system. The third category of role usage is applicable here when viewed "as the structural or normative elements defining behavior expected of role incumbents or actors, that is, their mutual rights and obligations" (Getzels, Lipham, and Campbell, 1968, p. 60). In this conceptualization, role has several notable characteristics which include "positions, offices, or statuses within an institution . . . are defined in terms of expectations . . . are institutional givens . . . , are more or less flexible . . . , are complementary . . . , and vary in scope" (Getzels, Lipham, and Campbell, 1968, pp. 60-64). Thus, roles are seen as the structure by which behaviors of role incumbents are defined. As a group and within the social system, Third Party Intervention practices adhere to these formulations and, when given appropriate direction and nurturing, such groups perform within reasonable expectations.

The third component of the social system within this theoretical formulation is expectations. Expectations are defined as the "rights and duties, privileges and obligations; . . . those prescriptions . . . that delineate what a person should and should not do under various circumstances as the incumbent of a particular role in a social system" (Getzels, Lipham, and Campbell, 1968, pp. 60-64). Sarbin (1954) supported this view: "A position in a social structure is equivalent to an organized system of role expectations" (pp. 225-226).

Social systems and role theory provide useful theoretical frameworks for a rational discussion of Third Party Intervention as it relates to educational decision-making. With proper development, Third Party Intervention activities can result in an educational enterprise pluralistically inclined and keenly sensitive to the needs of a broader range of the support and constituency spectrum of the school. Endeavors of this nature, when given constructive, patient, consistent, and effective leadership, can produce a community climate conducive to change, adaptation, and experimentation within a traditionally closed system (the school system). Third Party Intervention practices, when viewed from a social system theoretical basis, assure a greater degree of exchange of idea and concerns, and increase community, agency, and institutional collaboration in problem-solving and conflict management/resolution. This constitutes a major philosophical tenet of community education. The process, elaborated upon in discussions which follow, insures broad patron and advocate input in what Snyder (1958) referred to as "discrimination of relevancies . . . the selection and valuation of objects, events, symbols, conditions, and actors. These relevancies are, so to speak, carved from a total number of phenomena present in the overall setting" (p. 17).

Thus, as it relates to social systems theory, Third Party Intervention as herein discussed provides the school system with a highly visible, highly respected, and creditable mechanism for significant systems adaptation. In this regard, Easton (1965), a leading political systems analyst, asserted that "for any social system . . . adaptation represents more than simple adjustments to the events in its life. It is made up of efforts, limited only by the variety of human skills, resources, and ingenuity, to control, modify, or fundamentally change either the environment or the system itself, or both together" (pp. 20-21).

No significant and lasting change can evolve unless, as Mann (1975) has asserted, people commit their time, energy, skills, and creative resources to a common end. To quote Mann (1975):

> . . . when people orient themselves to a . . . school or school system, they do so with respect to three objects for their support. They can offer support first to the authorities, second to the regime, and third to the community. . . The authorities as an object of support simply refers to the system's decision-making role positions and their incumbents . . . "Regime" refers to the set of rules and structures through which inputs are transformed . . . Regime manifestations include by-laws, rules, regulations, customs, norms, doctrines, and values. The configuration of bureaucracy resident in any given school system is a regime . . . Together these regime aspects make up a distribution of power and authority . . . The third object of . . . support is that of "community". At its simplest, "community" is "we-feeling." (pp. 59-77)

The community, as used here, includes the entire make-up of the school community — teachers, principal, students, parents, agencies, businesses, churches, and non-school affiliated adults. Easton (1965) defined community as "a universal readiness or ability to continue working together to solve . . . problems" (p. 172). It is obvious that Third Party Intervention practices have the potential to engender adamant support at all three levels — authorities, regime, and community.

The following discussions further buttress this point of view and distinguishes Third Party Intervention Groups from traditional community advisory councils. It is the opinion of the authors that Community Advisory Councils have been ineffective in bringing about real changes in education systems and other community organizations.

During the late 1960's and early 1970's much emphasis was placed on the community control issue as it related to community participation. Some community educators argued that community control of local educational efforts was too disruptive to the educational system and the community. Others favored the community control model. It seems that there is some agreement that realistic community involvement must be insured. However, the problem lies in the fact that most education systems are closed to realistic community involvement. In those systems where community councils, task forces, or commissions do exist, their roles are restricted to the point where they are ineffective. There is much confusion regarding role and function even where specific objectives or purposes are outlined. These groups are also restricted to dealing with the problems of the organization, whether it be the school system or some agency.

While traditional, limited citizen involvement seems to have been ineffective, Third Party Intervention Groups have the potential to bring about substantive changes in community systems and inter-organizational relationships. Focus here is on citizen activity, a particular type of citizen participation that is devoted to problem-solving of community-wide issues, as distinct from simple analysis, and to the advancement of recommendations to a particular agency. It is a different form of citizens' activity and requires a different set of skills on the part of those who would choose to work in such a collaborative enterprise with all kinds of groups, particularly school officials.

Examples of such groups include the Management Review Committee of Los Angeles, The Dallas Alliance, The Council on Education in Kansas City, The San Francisco Public Schools Commission, and The Citizens Education Task Force of St. Louis.

These groups are usually citizen-initiated, have diverse memberships, substantial financial support, and small staffs. The essential difference between them and district-wide advisory councils lies in their level of activity and their public credibility. The strength of these Third Party, or third sector, groups lies in the fact that they are autonomous, that is, not attached to the school system or to any other agency. This factor allows for flexibility in determining the degree of involvement in any important issue confronting the community. Though many exist for only short periods of time, it is becoming more common for such groups to be on-going. Such Third Party Groups are not anti-establishment; they are not devoted to revolution; they are not fool-proof, absolute mechanisms for problem-solving; they are not short-termed, "easy in" and "easy out" groups; and they are not always limited to one area of public problems.

What are the functions to be performed by groups of this sort in community education? One of them is to work collaboratively with school authorities in the choice of problems to be approached, to prioritize among those and to share in the problem-defining and problem-solving processes. Another essential function is to extend community awareness regarding the problems of educational systems and the community at large; to speak to their seriousness, and to find ways and means to attack those problems which extend beyond the capabilities of the established institutions. A third function is to convene. It means gathering a planned assembly of people for particular purposes. It means moving in where there is a leadership vacuum. A fourth function is to legitimize a system's direction, while a fifth function is to mobilize resources to allow systems or organizations to achieve their objectives (Cunningham, 1976). All of the above mentioned functions form the matrix by which a continuous process of community revitalization and reclamation can be formulated, and by which a sense of community can be sustained, particularly in urban areas.

Based on the discussions, it is believed that the Third Party Intervention theory holds much promise for community educators who are farsighted and willing to take risks. If it is a necessity for community educators to assert themselves in pursuing more substantive goals, in addressing community revitalization and human reclamation, in bringing about "a sense of community," in addressing those problems which have direct bearing on the life-chances (those things and conditions which have direct influence upon survival) of individuals and or communities, Third Party Intervention Groups ought to be pursued by community education professionals. In order to delve into issues of broader community concern, it is essential that community educators at all levels attack those problems from a broader institutional base than the school. These other bases include business coalitions, government-industry-community coalitions, and coalitions of neighborhood and civic organizations. Ralph Nader (1977) contends:

> The era of wholesale delegation by citizens of their rights and hopes to unresponsive and indentured bureaucracy — government and corporate — is over. The emergence of neighborhood communities and functional citizen organizations along consumer, environmental and taxpayer lines is rapidly becoming one of America's greatest untold stories. The theme is direct democracy and the motif is the assumption of civic obligation by citizens themselves for the design of their future. (p. 8)

Community educators should be in the vangard of this kind of movement, for it would place them in the center of the action with the people.

REFERENCES

Bayham, D. The Great Cities Project. In E. Keach, R. Fulton, and W. E. Gardner (editors), *Education and social crisis*. New York: John Wiley and Sons, 1967.

Carr, L. J. *Analytical sociology*. New York: Harper and Rose, 1955.

Cunningham, L. *Problem-solving citizens' groups: A new forum of citizen involvement*. Paper presented at the meeting of the Third Party Intervention Association, San Francisco, May 1976.

Easton, D. *A systems analysis of political life*. New York: John Wiley and Sons, 1965.

Fantini, M. D. Implementing Equal Educational Opportunity. *Harvard Educational Review*, 1968, 38 (160-175).

Getzels, J. W. Conflict and Role Behavior in the Educational Setting. In W. W. Charters (editors), *Readings in the Social-Psychology of Education*. Boston: Allyn and Bacon, 1963.

Getzels, J. W. and Guba, E. G. Social behavior and the Administrative Process. *School Review*, 1957, 65, (423-441).

Getzels, J. W., Lipham, J. M., and Campbell, R. F. *Educational administration as a social process*. New York: Harper and Row, 1968.

Himes, J. S. *The study of sociology: An introduction*. Glenview, Illinois, Scott, Foresman and Co., 1968.

Lipham, J. M. Leadership and Administration. In D. E. Griffiths (editor), *Behavioral Science and Educational Administration*, Sixty-third Yearbook of the National Society for the Study of Education. Chicago: NSSE (distributed University of Chicago Press), 1964.

Mann, D. *Policy decision-making in education: An introduction to calculation and control*. New York: Teachers College Press, 1975.

Nader, R. Cited in C. S. Mott Foundation, *For Your Information, #6* (March 31, 1977), 8. Flint, Michigan: C. S. Mott Foundation, 1977.

Parsons, T. Suggestions for a Sociological Approach to the Theory of Organizations, I. *Administrative Science Quarterly*, 1956, 1(1), (63-85).

Parsons, T. Suggestions for a Sociological Approach to the Theory of Organizations, II. *Administrative Science Quarterly*, 1956, 1(2), (225-239).

Sarbin, T. R. Role Theory. In G. Lindzey (editor), *Handbook of Social Psychology*. Reading, Massachusetts: Addison-Welsey, 1954.

Snyder, R. C. A Decision-Making Approach to the Study of Political Phenomena. In R. Young (editor), *Approaches to the Study of Politics*. Evanston: Northwestern University Press, 1958.

"Grantsmanship/fund raising is a series of skills that must be developed with carefully-followed strategies to insure success." — Fish

Chapter 19

Grantsmanship/ Fund Raising Strategies

by

Thomas L. Fish

GRANTSMANSHIP/FUND RAISING STRATEGIES

INTRODUCTION

A successful community educator more often than not is a successful fundraiser who has developed grantsmanship and fundraising strategy skills to a high level of competence. Often this is done out of necessity as declining enrollments and inflation eat away at the general fund of most school systems. Increased pressure on general funds results in the attitude among many districts that community education is fine as long as it pays its own way. It can only be assumed that this attitude will continue to prevail for the foreseeable future, and thus, the skills for raising funds will become more, not less, important.

Successful fundraising strategy begins with a basic three-pronged tenet of community education: that needs must be identified; resources must be assessed; and finally, the appropriate need must be matched with the appropriate resource to solve the problem. Fundraising is most successful if this same process is followed.

This reading proceeds on the assumption that the need for funds has been clearly identified in specifics, that is, the community educator has gone beyond the statement that "Funds are needed for community education programs," to identify specific purposes for which money is needed — advisory council inservice training, senior citizen center, pre-school program, etc. This is a major assumption because this step is often overlooked in the fundraising strategy. Yet without it, success is highly unlikely. Only by knowing the purposes for which funds are sought can one seek out the appropriate source of funds.

This reading will deal with the strategies for identifying the appropriate funding sources and for securing those funds. Initially, the process of proposal writing will be considered, followed by strategies for identifying grant sources, both governmental and foundations.

PROPOSAL WRITING

The process of proposal writing is dealt with first because it is such an important skill in obtaining grants. Almost all foundations and governmental funding sources require the submission of a proposal to request funds. Although the actual format for proposals varies greatly from foundation to foundation and from governmental unit to governmental unit, all proposals contain the following nine components suggested by the Grantsmanship Center (Kiritz):

While the Proposal Summary should be the last thing written, it should be remembered that, in all likelihood, it will be the first thing read. Thus, it is essential that this section be as clear and succinct as possible. The goal of the summary should be to attract the reader's interest and convey to the reader exactly what it is that the project is to accomplish so that the reader will want to proceed with the reading of the entire proposal.

The introduction of any proposal should be used to establish credibility for the fund seeker and his/her organization. Reputations are important in receiving grants. As the saying goes, "The rich get richer" so, too, does the successful grantsperson who gets the first grant and handles it well. He/she is much more likely to get the second, third, etc. Thus, it is important to use this section to build the case as to why this fund seeker and his/her organization are capable of, and qualified to, carry out the program or project for which support is requested. Addressing the grant seeker directly, the Grantsmanship Center (Kiritz) suggests that the following be included in this introduction:

How you got started.

How long you have been around.

Anything unique about the way you got started, or the fact that you were the first thus-and-so organization in the country, etc.

Some of your most significant accomplishments as an organization, or if you are a new organization, some of the significant accomplishments of your Board or Staff in their previous roles.

Your organizational goals — why you were started.

What support you have received from other organizations and prominent individuals (accompanied by some letters of endorsement which can be in an appendix). (p. 2)

These letters of endorsement should indicate what the organization or individual will do to assist the project, and should not be just general letters of support.

Having established credibility, it is necessary in the Problem Statement to clearly define the problem which is being addressed for solution. This problem should be very specific and documented with evidence of a needs assessment, if possible. Many people tend to state the problem too broadly, and as a result, they identify an unmanageable problem. The three key points to be included in this section are:

Make a logical connection between your organization's background and the problems and needs with which your purpose to work.

Support the existence of the problem by evidence. Statistics . . . are but one type of support. You may also get advice from groups in the community concerned about the problem, from prospective clients, and from other organizations working in the community and professionals in the field.

Define clearly the problems with which you intend to work. Make sure that what you want to do is workable — that it can be done within a reasonable time, by you, and with a reasonable amount of money. (Kiritz, p. 3)

Program Objectives form the next component of a good proposal. Objectives can be defined as the intended results of the project. The objectives should be measureable, they should have a completion time, and they should have criteria for success. It is necessary that they emanate from the problem which was defined in the previous section — that is, the objectives should alleviate the identified problem.

Methods form the fifth important aspect of a good proposal. Methods, very succinctly, are those things to be accomplished in order to achieve the objectives. They are the tactics, strategies or schemes that will be implemented to actually alleviate the problems that have been identified. In this section of a proposal, related literature is most important. What have others tried? How is this project different or better? How will it work? What must be attempted here is to build a case for the methods being selected as well as to demonstrate knowledge of other attempts to deal with the same or similar problems.

It should be pointed out that methods are discrete from objectives. One way that this distinction can be easily remembered is that objectives are the results or outcomes of efforts (methods). Methods are in the inputs or procedures that will be utilized to achieve a certain result.

Evaluation strategies form the next important component of a good proposal. Yet, based on the author's experience as a reader of both federal and state proposals, evaluation consistently is one of the weakest aspects of most proposals. Any funding source wants to know how the grantees will know that they have achieved what it was that they set out to do. If the objectives have been carefully thought out so that they truly are measure-able, so that they do have a completion time and criteria for success, then the evaluation section of a proposal is very easy to write.

If, however, objectives are not clear and do not possess those three necessary characteristics, then evaluation is most difficult, and for all practical purposes is impossible. When this occurs, proposal writers tend to write in that "surveys will be taken to see how people feel about the project." Feelings are nice, but funding sources are interested in hard data that objectively indicate that a problem has been solved. After all, that was the reason for the request for financial support in the first place.

Future funding is an oft neglected component, yet one which is essential. No funding source is interested in maintaining a program or project indefinitely, nor are they interested in starting a project that will cease to function in one, two or three years after the initial funding expires. It is important, therefore, that a section of the proposal deal with ways that the project will be financially maintained in the future.

Last, but not least, is the budget. A budget is a financial picture of the project. The items should be related to the methods described in the proposal. A reader should be able to readily discern the relationship between the budget and the objectives and methods being undertaken. There should also be evidence of matching or inkind support for the project so that it is not totally a "soft" money project. Finally, it is essential to break each item down into its components so that the reader can readily see the items that make up each component. For example, do not state "Salaries - $24,000," but rather, "two certified teachers at $12,000 each."

The following budget worksheet should be helpful in planning a budget.

	Grant	Match
A. *Staff Compensation*		
Professional Staff	_____	_____
Clerical Staff	_____	_____
Other Staff	_____	_____
Total Staff	_____	_____
B. *Fringe Benefits*		
Retirement Plan	_____	_____
Social Security	_____	_____
Health Benefits	_____	_____
Life Insurance	_____	_____
Other Benefits	_____	_____
Total Benefits	_____	_____

	Grant	Match
C. *Consultants*		
Consultant	_____	_____
Total Consultant	_____	_____
D. *Supplies*		
Office Supplies	_____	_____
Program Supplies	_____	_____
Telephone	_____	_____
Postage	_____	_____
Other Supplies	_____	_____
Total Supplies	_____	_____
E. *Equipment*		
Purchase	_____	_____
Rental	_____	_____
Lease	_____	_____
Total Equipment	_____	_____
F. *Space*		
Rent	_____	_____
Utilities	_____	_____
Maintenance	_____	_____
Total Space	_____	_____
G. *Travel*		
Local	_____	_____
Out of Town	_____	_____
Total Travel	_____	_____
H. *Professional Development*	_____	_____
Conferences	_____	_____
Subscriptions	_____	_____
Dues & Memberships	_____	_____
Staff Training	_____	_____
Other	_____	_____
Total Professional Development		
I. *Evaluation*	_____	_____
J. *Other*		
Printing	_____	_____
Other	_____	_____
Total Other	_____	_____
GRANT TOTAL	_____	_____

Finally, in the proposal writing process it must be emphasized that the most important aspect of a proposal is the problem statement. If the problem is clearly defined and narrowed down from a global situation to one which is manageable, then the other components of the proposal flow naturally from the problem.

The process of writing a good proposal is followed by the task of identifying the proper agency or group to approach. It is on that task of source location that this discussion will now focus.

GOVERNMENTAL SOURCES

There are four levels of governmental sources of support. These levels are: local; county; state; and federal. The fund seeker must evaluate each of these levels to determine which is the most appropriate source. To identify these potential sources, the fund raiser should contact key individuals at each level of government. It is important to get to know personally, or get to know someone who does personally know such individuals as commissioners, state legislators and state department personnel. Most funds which flow at these levels come as a result of personal contacts which alert potential fundees of the availability of funds. Each community, county, and state organization is different, but the need for personal contact with the funding source is always the same. It is crucial.

Obviously, identifying potential sources of funds at the federal level is much more difficult, due to the vastness of governmental programs and the lack of personal contacts. Therefore, the fund seeker must find alternative ways to gain accurate information about current federal programs. There are three particular strategies for doing this that the author has found most beneficial.

The first is to gain access to *The Catalog of Federal Domestic Assistance*. This publication is basic for anyone in search of federal assistance. One word of warning must be kept in mind. Even though the Catalog lists over 1000 federal assistance programs, it is not complete and not totally accurate. All agencies are requested to submit the necessary information, but it is not mandatory that they do so. As a result, the information can only serve as a starting point in the search. It is, however, a major help in getting that start because the *Catalog* identifies the types of assistance programs available, program purposes, eligibility requirements as well as application procedures.

At the beginning of this publication are seven indices which allow the grantsperson who has very little information from which to start to find a particular program. The seven indices are:

1. Agency index, which identifies each program accordingly to its administering agency.
2. Individual index, which identifies those programs for which an individual may apply.
3. State index, which identifies those programs for which a state government may apply.
4. Local index, which lists those programs for which local governments may apply.
5. Functional index, which lists programs according to 18 categories.
6. Popular name index, which identifies programs according to their popular name.
7. Subject index, which identifies programs according to subject.

These indices are followed by *Program Changes,* which are the deletions, additions, and changes to programs. Having once studied the *Catalog,* one need to only annually review this section of each new edition to keep current regarding possible assistance programs.

The meat of the *Catalog* are the Program Descriptions' sections which compose the bulk of the publication. Important information is provided for each program listed, such as objectives of program; type of assistance; user and use restrictions; eligibility and application processes; financial information; regulations; contact personnel; and related programs.

A supplement to this Catalog is published once a year in an attempt to keep the publication current, but this is a difficult task. The next two strategies are particularly suited to dealing with this keeping-up-to-date problem once an individual is familiar with *The Catalog of Federal Domestic Assistance.*

The second strategy for identifying sources of funds at the federal level is to gain access to a subscription of the *Federal Register.* The *Federal Register* is a daily publication, excepting weekends, to which many schools and public libraries regularly subscribe. A request to the librarian usually makes them available. The issues of the *Federal Register* need only be scanned daily to keep current with the new legislation funding programs, public hearings, and opportunities for comment concerning proposed regulations for new programs, as well as announcements of RFP's (Request for Proposals) with deadline dates. Scanning the *Federal Register* may appear to be a time consuming task since it is a daily task, but it does pay off.

The third strategy for identifying sources and also for remaining current is to subscribe to a service which can, and will, furnish speedy and accurate information concerning current federal programs. There are many of these services which have weekly newsletters to subscribers as well as telephone access to assist the subscriber in finding the accurate information in the least possible time. One of these services which the author recommends is:

Education Funding Research Council
752 National Press Building, N.W.
Washington, D.C. 20045
(202) 347-6342

Once an appropriate program has been identified at the federal level, it is necessary to work to build that personal contact with people within that funding agency as recommended with the local, county, and state levels of government. Careful attention must be given to deadlines as well.

FOUNDATIONS

Foundations constitute another important potential source of funds for community education programs (Fish & Klassen, 1976). There are five types of foundations of which the fundraiser should be aware (Shakely, 1977). The first is national foundations. These are the foundations such as the Ford Foundation. To be of interest to this type of foundation, the project must have national implications.

The second type of foundation is the special interest foundation, such as the Robert Johnson Foundation which has a special interest in health. A project must deal with their special interest in order for them to consider that request.

The third type of foundation is the family foundation, such as the Hill Family Foundation. These often are interested in the community and often give most of their grants to the local area. These are excellent sources if there is one located in the project area.

The corporate foundations constitute the fourth type of foundation. The Ford Motor Fund is an example of this type. These foundations are pass-throughs for the corporation. If there is a plant or corporation of this type in the project area, it would be wise to investigate this possibility.

The fifth type of foundation is the community foundation, such as the Minneapolis Foundation. These are really public charities and are an excellent source for community education support because they are restricted by law to keep their grants within the community which they serve.

There are over 25,000 foundations in the United States in these five categories. Of these 25,000, approximately 13,000 actually make grants. In 1976 these foundations made grants of approximately two billion dollars. Compared with the over 35 billion dollars that the Department of Health,

Education and Welfare alone distributed that same year, it is obvious that foundations are not a major source of funds. However, they are a very important source since they are willing to risk their money on new programs which, if successful, can often lead to governmental support.

As with governmental sources, the key to being successful in generating foundation support is to have a strategy that leads to the right foundation. How does one find out about the foundations? One of the easiest ways is to become aware of The Foundation Center. The Center is a non-profit organization whose primary purposes are to be a useful resource for anyone interested in applying to grant-making foundations for funds and to provide reliable information on foundations. Interested persons should contact:

The Foundation Center
1001 Connecticut Avenue, N.W.
Washington, D. C. 20036

One of the major services of The Foundation Center is the maintenance of libraries relative to foundations. Information is provided free of charge to library visitors. Fees are charged, however, for most information service by mail, telephone, etc.

In addition to two Foundation Center libraries maintained in New York and Washington, D. C., there are 49 regional libraries located in 39 states. These regional libraries are particularly important for those seeking detailed information. These collections contain many reference works, books, foundation reports, annual reports and other information pertaining to individual foundations.

For areas that are not convenient to these national libraries or any of the 49 regional libraries, there are hundreds of college, university and public libraries across the United States which provide information concerning foundations as well.

A person seeking foundation support needs to know which foundations are available. The individual fund seeker should turn to one of these libraries and consult *The Foundation Directory*. There are several editions of this directory, the latest being Edition 6, published in 1977, which lists all of the major foundations in the United States with assets over one million dollars or which make grants of over $500,000 annually. *The Foundation Directory* lists in excess of 2,500 foundations. These foundations are listed by state, with each foundation's address listed. Also, for each foundation, the following information is given: the donors; the purpose and activities; financial data, including assets, gifts received, expenditures, etc.; the officers of the foundation; the trustees of the foundation.

The Foundation Directory is extremely important because it gives the fund seeker an idea of the broad purposes of the foundation. Thus, it helps the individual narrow the list of foundations which might potentially be interested in his or her project.

A second source which the potential fund seeker should consult is *The Foundation Directory Supplement.* The supplement provides additional information, such as bibliographic materials, which one might consult. More importantly, however, *The Foundation Directory Supplement* provides a list of smaller foundations, such as those which have assets of under one million dollars or which grant less than $500,000 annually. Most people are not aware that there are so many foundations within individual states. In the state of Minnesota, for example, a state which has under four million people, there are over 300 foundations. Seventy-five of those foundations are listed in *The Foundation Directory.* The others are listed in *The Foundation Directory Supplement.* New York State has in excess of 3,000 foundations, and Colorado has in excess of 100 foundations. Thus, it can be seen that many foundations which are potential sources of funds are readily overlooked if one does not consult both sources.

A third important source which individuals should consult for foundation information is *The Foundation News.* This bimonthly publication features articles about individual foundations and the types of grants that they are giving. More importantly, however, to the individual seeking funds is to be found in a 3-part section of *The Foundation News* entitled "The Foundation Grants Index." Section I of this index lists foundations alphabetically and the grants which they have made during the two-month period which *The Foundation News* covers. Section II lists the recipients of the grants, and Section III provides a list of descriptive words or phrases under which the grant was given. For example, in "The Foundation Grants Index" of *The Foundation News,* September-October 1975, there were two grants given under the category of "Education (Community)." This immediately identifies two foundations which might be interested in community education activities.

One other important resource that should be utilized by the grant seeker is the *Grantsmanship Center News.* The Grantsmanship Center is located in Los Angeles, California. It is a nonprofit educational institution which is primarily interested in providing resources for grantspersons. *The Grantsmanship Center News,* published eight times a year, is an excellent magazine concerning all facets of grantsmanship. It identifies foundations, critques proposals, and provides another source of information for the individual seeking foundation as well as governmental sources of support.

Having identified several foundations which might be interested in the project for which support is being sought, it is important at this point for fund seekers to visit the foundations and talk with their staffs about the particular community education project under consideration. This is best done personally, if that is possible; if not, a telephone call will suffice. By talking to the staff members of the foundation and explaining the proposal for funding, the staff, in turn, can give some indication whether or not they would be interested in supporting the project. If the foundation has been carefully researched prior to this step by the fund seeker regarding locale, size, purposes, and activities, the chances are good that the foundation's program officer will be willing to listen to the fund raisers' proposal. This is particularly true of family operated foundations which are primarily interested in having an impact on a local area. Since most community education programs would be seeking funds for programs to impact a local area, it is essential that fund seekers do their homework prior to their foundation visit.

The program officer will, at this time, be able to provide the necessary instructions and selection criteria which the foundation has established relative to proposals. It is essential that these instructions and criteria be carefully studied and that enough planning be completed to allow sufficient time for meeting deadline dates.

Once the planning stage of seeking grants has been carried out, the only task remaining is the actual preparation of the proposal itself. The proposal format will vary from foundation to foundation. Thus, it is essential that this information be obtained from the program officer at the time of the initial meeting.

The actual proposal development process is the same as outlined above for both governmental sources and foundations.

One final comment regarding both foundation and governmental sources of support. It is essential that the fund seeker not be disappointed if the proposal is not funded. Ninety percent of all proposals submitted to public and private sources are rejected. Should a proposal fall within this ninety percent, contact the governmental agency or foundation and ask for some feedback as to why the proposal was rejected. Once this feedback is received, it often is possible to make changes and to resubmit the proposal at a later date. It has been found that resubmissions have the same chance of funding as the original proposal submission. Remember, however, if there has been adequate preparation in identifying the proper agency/foundation for the proposal, the odds are greatly enhanced from the one chance out of ten that is the norm.

By way of conclusion, grantsmanship/fund raising is a series of skills that successful community educators must sharpen. Furthermore, strategies must be developed and carefully followed to insure success. The foregoing pages have laid out some successful strategies for two sources of support, governmental and foundations. Other strategies need to be developed for other potential sources of funds as well.

REFERENCES

Fish, T. L., and Klassen, J. A. *Financing community education.* Midland, Michigan: Pendell Publishing Co., 1976.

Kiritz, N. J. Program planning and proposal writing. *The Grantsmanship Center News,* undated, 1-8.

Shakely, J. *Grantsmanship.* Paper presented at the Grantsmanship Training Program, St. Paul, April, 1977.

"It is common to hear community educators talk of one of community education's more universal and ambitious goals, which is to identify and develop indigenous leadership in the community. Apropos of this goal, it appears that one path toward its realization may be to engage a community's citizens in the evaluation process as often and in as many ways as possible." — *Vaught*

CHAPTER 20

Evaluation Strategies in Community Education

by

Lee K. Vaught

EVALUATION STRATEGIES IN COMMUNITY EDUCATION

INTRODUCTION

Practitioners in community education appear to be fully cognizant of the critical role that evaluation should and must assume if community education is to make the difference in quality of life that is so often, if not openly claimed, certainly implied by its proponents. Given the fact that an urgent need does exist and is recognized by many practitioners, the obvious question that comes to mind is: Why does the need, if determined to be genuine by many persons in the field, continue to go unattended? A possible answer might be found in a suggestion made by Steele (1975) who speaks of the "mystique of evaluation" and its resultant tendency to intimidate. The negative connotation traditionally associated with evaluation, with its oft perceived purpose of weeding out or unseating the unworthy or incompetent is, because of its pervasiveness, a difficult perspective to transcend despite all the quality work that has been done in recent years to alter this mentality. Although much progress has been made toward changing this view to one that is positive in terms of evaluation's potential as a growth facilitating process, the transition is not yet complete.

The intent of the following pages is to provide some documentation to support the view that evaluation in community education does, in fact, need sustained attention. They will suggest some strategies that might help community educators to become more comfortable with evaluation and move closer to making the process a vital, consumer-oriented dimension of community education.

THE NEED FOR EVALUATION IN COMMUNITY EDUCATION

In the course of reviewing what various people, including some notables, have to say on the subject of evaluation in community education, one is both enlightened and confounded. One piece seems to give order to the reader's understanding while another tends, mostly, to confuse. This perceptual disparity notwithstanding, the reviewer finds nearly all writers agreeing that the need for sustained attention to evaluation in community education is urgent. Furthermore, suggested approaches are more alike than different. While terminology, various emphases, and sequence of events in the process or the precise manner in which it is to be done vary, there is little variance over the belief that sound and defensible evaluation procedures are, by and large, non-existent in community education. Perhaps it is safer to say that the incidence of competent evaluation practice is less prominent than that of perfunctory or self-serving effort.

Theoreticians and practitioners alike seem to be in general agreement on the need for legitimizing the evaluation dimension of community education. Certainly, the scrutiny to which the movement is subject today mandates that evaluation become an area of prime concern among professionals in the field. They continue to seek, fundamentally, to establish community education's merit as judged by the institutions and agencies whose support is essential to the movement's survival.

A national study of evaluation practice in community education (Boyd, 1975) funded by the U.S. Office of Education reviewed evaluation efforts of local educational agencies, state departments of education, and institutions of higher education. Some of the findings at the local educational agency level are particularly interesting. While space does not permit the detailing of findings here, some of the prevailing conditions at that time, which Boyd saw fit to report, were:

1. There is little, if any, relationship between locally stated objectives and evaluation of participant satisfaction, personnel performance, or program outcome.
2. Most evaluations are, to use terms suggested by Scriven (1972, pp. 28-29) of a *formative* rather than *summative* type.
3. Local educational agencies often use evaluation to serve program purposes having little to do with evaluation, such as one of broadening the scope of citizen involvement, of raising consciousness of the program, or of interacting with key people in the community, hoping thereby to stimulate support for the program.
4. There is a scarcity of performance criteria that can be measured in objective terms.
5. Performance "findings" tend often to be consensual judgments resulting from discussion among evaluators; this occurring in both internal and external evaluations.
6. Selection of objectives tends to focus on ease of measurement rather than on their value in achievement. As a consequence, objectives are often trivial in nature.
7. A general lack of clarity exists in distinguishing between measures of program performance and program outcome.

In sum, Boyd calls attention to an urgent need for community educators to find ways by which existing confusion might be cleared up and acceptable methods devised for measuring outcome.

A few writers and some authorities have begun to focus seriously on the need for improved evaluation strategies and, particularly, for including citizens in the process. Relating specifically to the citizen participation dimension, Provus (1973) writes:

> When participants are directly involved in the evaluation of an educational program, the apathetic turn interested, the militant turn constructive, and all achieve heightened sensitivity. When a school neighborhood is involved in evaluation, parents, educators, and community resource people establish mutual respect and a broader vision of the possible. (p. 660)

While most writers simply concur on the notion that its a good idea, a few suggest specific ways in which citizens might be involved in the process. Certain approaches and recommendations that seem especially appropriate for community education are discussed briefly in the following section. The focus will not be one of detailing the complexities of evaluation systems. Rather, it will attempt to convey the essence of potentially useful models and studied viewpoints in hopes that some direction for community leadership in evaluation will emerge.

COMMUNITY LEADERSHIP POTENTIAL IN EVALUATIONS

Stufflebeam (1975) advises community educators to be aware of two main purposes to be served by evaluation: one of *decision-making*; the other of *accountability*. He builds a case for the importance of both dimensions to the realization of a productive evaluation effort. Although a clear distinction is drawn between planning and implementation on the one hand and analysis and appraisal of outcome on the other, a certain interdependence may be inferred that is useful to the person seeking to understand relationships among the numerous elements of evaluation.

The Context, Input, Process, Product (CIPP) Model conceptualized by Stufflebeam (1971) has considerable potential for use by the community educator in determining a clear and logical flow for the evaluation process. Moreover, possibilities for its use in engaging community leadership in the evaluation process are myriad. Of the four types of evaluation described in the CIPP Model, its designer considers Context Evaluation to be the most basic type. It defines the relevant environment or setting in which evaluation is to take place. The Context Evaluation describes conditions as they are as well as what they might optimally be. It identifies needs as well as resources that might be brought to bear on meeting identified needs. Still another function is that of defining obstructions that stand in the way of resolving problems and meeting the needs of people and communities. Context Evaluation is particularly useful in its application to the definition of values and goals of the system or program that is to be evaluated. Stufflebeam sees the methodology of Context Evaluation being applied to the system in two ways: 1) in the contingency mode, which seeks external means to improve the setting or environment and, 2) in the congruence mode where a comparison is made between actual and intended performance of the system. Simply stated, the contingency mode seeks improvement while congruence endeavors to gain conformance. Seemingly at odds with each other, a closer look reveals that the two modes are complementary in at least one fundamental way. For long-range improvement to occur, present quality of activity must be good. It follows that there must always be an effort to improve on what is being done. Community educators need congruence evaluation to keep check on whether they are, indeed, doing what they intended and said they would do. Contingency evaluation is equally important by virtue of its value in responding appropriately to changes occurring in communities being served.

Remaining components of the CIPP Model (Input, Process, and Product) will not be discussed here, except to say that each constitutes an essential element in the total evaluation effort and should be studied carefully by those interested in or concerned with current evaluation practice in community education. Overall, the implications of Stufflebeam's model for the direct and vital involvement of a community's citizens in the evaluation process are countless. In fact it is probable that a decision to include or exclude the lay-citizen participation dimension could spell the difference between success or failure in its application to evaluation in community education. Similarly, much of the leadership necessary to evaluate a program efficiently exists in abundant supply in the typical community. Of course, such leadership is often latent and may forever remain so without a specific effort to energize it — to allow it to manifest itself and become a vital force in creating or improving community. The lay/professional mix in typical community citizenship provides a vast resource of the most comprehensive sort. Combined perspectives inherent therein would provide a dimension in the evaluation process that would be otherwise unobtainable. To be sure, there will be perceptual differences and diversity of opinion. However, the process-oriented community educator is likely to see this as a golden opportunity for bringing citizens together to thrash out community issues and concerns and plan for community improvement through a sound evaluation strategy.

Provus (1971), in his Discrepancy Evaluation Model, speaks to judging performance against a standard. As others both before and after him have suggested, the standard against which performance and quality of output will be measured is, ultimately, the product of values held and goals sought by a given program's client population. It behooves the community leadership developer to engage those with a vested interest in their community in reaching as near consensus as possible on basic values, defining and setting goals, and determining the avenues most likely to be productive in reaching stated goals. The community educator should be operationally familiar with some of the group process systems that have been developed expressly for use in this effort. Hall's (1967) Goal Setting Process and Delargy's (1974) Community Education Goal Ascertainment Kit are but two examples of such systems that have been used successfully in the field. The Delphi Technique employed in the latter system is a particularly useful tool early in the evaluation process as it calls for involvement of group participants in deciding what is to be evaluated, how it is to be done and who is to play what role. The process is helpful, also, in underscoring the relevancy of evaluation and securing commitment to the process.

An evaluation model that should be of special interest to the community educator is one described by Brinkerhoff (1977, p. 97) in a recently published conference report. Derived from Provus' Evaluation Discrepancy Model, it provides a consumer-oriented framework for school program evaluation wherein the intent is to ascertain whether a given school program is doing what it purports to be doing by way of a rather unique public feed-back system. Essentially a public information-accountability model, it informs citizens about a given educational plan via public media, reports regularly to the public on progress in carrying out the plan and, finally, asks the public to rate how well the program seems to have accomplished what it set out to do. In Brinkerhoff's words:

> Public evaluation is fundamentally unique because it is a way of giving parents and other taxpayers information they have never before received. School evaluation information has traditionally tended to rise in the system; that is, it has been produced by experts in evaluation for other experts, such as program management and funding agencies. Public evaluation is a dramatic reversal of this flow; evaluative information is gathered by trained lay persons and given directly to the public.

The Public Evaluation model described appears to have considerable potential for use in community education. Most community educators, however, would agree that its defensibility as an evaluation technique in community education rests with the manner in which the programs under scrutiny have come to be. If citizens who are being asked to judge how well a program has done what its designers hoped it would do have been engaged instrumentally in the planning — and, yes, in the designing — of the effort, it is nearly assured that the outcome will be of value to those persons served. If not, its worth in advancing a community effort would be questionable if not counter-productive.

231

Additional support for client/consumer participation in evaluation was offered by Steele (1975) who insisted that a community's citizens can and should be involved to the maximum extent possible in every phase of the evaluation process. Earlier, Hammond (1973, p. 169) suggested, albeit guardedly, that local people might be trained to conduct the evaluation process. He saw appropriate training of interested citizens by evaluation specialists to be essential in order that a creditable job be done and, further, claimed that this would be an excellent way to involve citizens in the evaluation process.

Another interesting group process strategy was proposed by Welty (1972, p. 128) for community involvement in educational evaluation and planning. The plan includes calling together a number of persons who represent diverse interest groups in the community. The assembled group works with a professional evaluator in the development of an evaluation process. Representatives of the interest groups, teachers, community members and students are asked to express themselves about their conceptions of a given educational program. The evaluator asks a series of a very specific questions, recording responses that will be used to develop a rudimentary program design. Following an opportunity to review the first draft of the design, the representatives are again assembled, perhaps in another plenary session or possibly in sub-groups. This procedure is repeated as many times as all persons involved deem necessary to reach the degree of precision desired. It is the evaluator's hope, of course, that the sessions will provide the means to assemble information useful in preparation of program design. An additional function of the meeting, aside from that of information gathering, is to facilitate consensus building. Further group process strategies are employed in which the original planners work closely with the evaluator in determining program outcomes, recycling for program improvement, and assuring that all persons remain generally in touch with what is happening in relation to what was planned.

CONCLUSION

It is common to hear community educators talk of one of community education's more universal and ambitious goals, which is to identify and develop indigenous leadership in the community. Apropos of this goal, it appears that one path toward its realization may be to engage a community's citizens in the evaluation process as often and in as many ways as possible. Community educators know what success in an endeavor requires commitment and that commitment demands ownership. Furthermore, prerequisites to ownership are thorough knowledge and first-hand involvement as well as a self-perceived ability to contribute significantly to an effort.

Many of the human resources considered necessary to conceive, develop and operationalize a sound evaluation system are present in every community; admittedly, often unrefined and, in such state, unusable. The challenge for the community educator is to devise the means by which native human resources may be refined and put to use. The product of such effort will go far toward assuring that evaluation comes to be an integral part of the community education process and, in addition, that the community leadership element assumes its proper role in that process.

REFERENCES

Boyd, Arthur, *Evaluation Today in Community Education* (Community Education Advisory Council, Report No. 1). Washington, D.C.; Office of Education, United States Department of Health, Education and Welfare, 1976.

Brinkerhoff, Robert. Public Evaluation — An Overview, In C. Beegle & R. Edelfelt (Eds.), *Staff Development: Staff Liberation.* Washington, D.C.: Association for Supervision and Curriculum Development, 1977.

DeLargy, Paul. *Community Education Goal Ascertainment.* Midland, Michigan: Pendell Publishing Co., 1974.

Hall, Lacy & Billy Sharp. *Achievement Motivation Systems.* Chicago: W. Clement and Jessie V. Stone Foundation, 1967.

Hammond, Robert L. Evaluation at the Local Level. In B. Worthen & J. Sanders (Eds.), *Educational Evaluation: Theory and Practice.* Worthington, Ohio: Charles A. Jones Publishing Co., 1973.

Provus, Malcolm. *Discrepancy Evaluation.* Berkeley, California: McCutchan Publishing Corp., 1971.

————. In Search of Community. *Phi Delta Kappan,* 1973, 54.

Scriven, Michael. The Methodology of Evaluation. In P. Taylor & D. Cowley (Eds.), *Readings in Curriculum Evaluation.* Dubuque, Iowa: William C. Brown Co., 1972.

Steele, Marilyn. Citizen Participation in the Planning/Evaluation Process. *Community Education Journal*, 1975, 5 (2), 28.

Stufflebeam, Daniel L. Evaluation as a Community Education Process. *Community Education Journal*, 1975, 5 (2), 8.

Stufflebeam, Daniel L., et al. *Educational Evaluation and Decision Making.* Phi Delta Kappa National Study on Evaluation. Itasca, Illinois: F. E. Peacock Publishers, 1971.

Welty, Gordon. Evaluation and Planning in Education: A Community Concern. In P. Taylor & D. Cowley (Eds.), *Readings in Curriculum Evaluation.* Dubuque, Iowa: William C. Brown Co., 1972.

PART V

THE NATIONAL NETWORK FOR PROMOTION OF COMMUNITY EDUCATION

"Over the years, the Mott Foundation's involvement has spread from a local thrust of funding community education projects in Flint and throughout the state of Michigan to a national effort." — Gregg

Chapter 21

The National Network For Dissemination and Training Sponsored by the Mott Foundation

by

Gloria A. Gregg

THE NATIONAL NETWORK FOR DISSEMINATION AND TRAINING SPONSORED BY THE MOTT FOUNDATION

EARLY BEGINNINGS OF FOUNDATION INVOLVEMENT

Since its inception in 1926, the C. S. Mott Foundation has had a history of funding programs which were aimed at improving the quality of life of individuals and the communities in which they live. Foundation involvement with what has become known as the community education concept began in 1935. In that year, Frank J. Manley, a physical education supervisor with the Flint Community Schools, convinced C. S. Mott, founder of the Mott Foundation, to make a small grant to the Flint Board of Education for the purpose of keeping several schools open beyond the normal hours to provide recreation and enrichment opportunities for people of all ages. While Flint's lighted school concept was not the first documented community school (Olsen and Clark, 1977, p. 62), the Flint program soon became a catalyst and national model for community school development. Additionally, it was the first city system to go this route.

From this initial investment in Flint, the Foundation's philosophical and financial commitment to the development of community education has grown steadily. Over the years, the Foundation's involvement has spread from a local thrust of funding community education projects in Flint and throughout the state of Michigan to a national effort.

Foundation support for community education has taken a variety of forms. While it is not the intent of this author to discuss all projects funded by the Foundation, several projects important to the evolvement of community education nationally are worthy of mention. The establishment of the National Center for Community Education came about in response to the increasing need for trained leaders in community education. Since 1963, the Foundation has funded various training programs at the National Center in an effort to meet the ever increasing demand for trained community educators. In conjunction with the National Center for Community Education and seven Michigan colleges and universities, the Mott Inter-University Clinical Preparation Program was started in 1963. Each year, approximately seventy men and women from throughout the nation were selected to receive graduate fellowships to study in Flint, Michigan. This program was discontinued in 1974. For a number of years short-term training programs usually two to six weeks in length, have been sponsored by the Foundation. Since the Mott Inter-University Clinical Preparation Program ceased operation, two of these short-term programs have continued under the sponsorship of the Foundation. Eastern Michigan University directs a series of training programs for persons working in or about to be working in community education positions, and also sessions for selected students working on advanced degrees in education. The Foundation has also provided some financial assistance to the National Community Education Association especially during its early days of development. Also, beginning in 1958, the Foundation, in collaboration with the Flint Community Schools, has sponsored annual national workshops in Flint. These workshops, which are usually two-three days in length, have provided thousands of persons a chance to learn more about community education and to study the Flint model. Starting in 1974 for the first time, the fall workshop was held outside Flint with Minneapolis, Minnesota, serving as the host. Since then, Washington, D.C.; Salt Lake City, Utah; Birmingham, Alabama; St. Louis, Missouri; and San Diego, California have held the fall session with Flint still hosting the spring session. Finally, perhaps the Foundation project which has contributed most to the overall acceptance and progress of community education is the Foundation's plan for, and financial support of, a national network of regional and cooperating centers for community education development.

ESTABLISHMENT OF THE REGIONAL CENTER NETWORK

Over the years, more and more interest was shown nationally in the concept of community education, the need to devise a means to disseminate information and to train more community educators became evident. The Foundation responded to this need by establishing a network of fifteen regional centers for community education development. The location of these centers and the dates they were established are listed below:

1963-64 Northern Michigan University

1965-66 Alma College (Michigan)

1966-67 Ball State University (Indiana)
Florida Atlantic University
Western Michigan University

1967-68 Arizona State University
Brigham Young University (Utah)

1969-70 Eastern Michigan University

1970-71 Connecticut State College
(Transferred in 1972 to the
University of Connecticut)
San Jose State College
(Now named California State University)

1971-72 Texas A & M
         University of Alabama
         University of Virginia

1972-73 University of Florida
         University of Missouri — St. Louis

In most cases, each of the regional centers was given responsibility for community education in a multi-state area. Part of this responsibility was to include establishment of cooperating centers to serve each state or part of a state in the region. It was the intent of the Foundation that, as the total center network evolved, the geographic spread would assure adequate development of the community education concept throughout the nation. As of June, 1976, the yearly Foundation statistical report on community education reported 85 such centers in operation.

THE FIVE-YEAR PLAN AND CENTER DEVELOPMENT

In 1972, the Foundation recognized the need for developing a long range (five-year) plan in order to insure that the national goal of community education would be met.

The national goal of community education is to see that every school in the United States has the opportunity to become a community school in accordance with established definitions and criteria of community education. (C.S. Mott Foundation, 1972, p. 1)

While this goal was not necessarily reasonable for the Foundation to reach by itself, the regional center directors felt achievement was a possibility when Mott funds were multipled by other resources.

The major purpose for developing such a plan was to integrate the Foundation's various training and dissemination activities, programs and similar components into a total delivery system. An integral part of the plan was continued investment of Foundation resources into existing regional centers and possibly other agencies who were committed to the national goal and willing to work towards its implementation. In this way, the Foundation's leadership would serve as an incentive in the national development of community education.

In order to develop a long range plan such as the one proposed by the Foundation, a process was established which would extensively involve the personnel from the fifteen regional centers. The first step was to hold a series of regional meetings attended by the center personnel to explore, identify, and discuss those elements which might be necessary to the success of a national program to promote the community education concept. The

241

results of these meetings were compiled into a set of guidelines which were then used by each regional center as a basis for developing its own five year plan.

From the plans prepared by each center, the Foundation staff attempted to identify common elements and multipliers which could be used to derive a Foundation plan. This phase of planning was followed by a meeting of all center directors where all material and information gathered and developed to date was discussed. The summation of these reports and opinions were then used to develop a series of questions to which each center director responded. These responses together with the previously prepared materials were then used as a basis for developing a final five-year plan.

In commenting on the five year plan projection upon its completion, the Foundation staff (1972) stated:

> We recognize, therefore, that the master plan we are now recommending is not an inalterable prescription for the future. At first glance, it may seem complicated, but it should be viewed as a broad framework on which we hope and intend to build. Inherent in long-range planning is the basic principle that it should not become fossilized, and that it is subject to review and updating each year. We intend, therefore, that each year's plan will be current, strategic and fully operational in concept and character. (p. 3)

Within the five-year plan, which covers the fiscal years 1973-78, three primary functions for the centers were delineated. The first function, dissemination, refers to those activities related to making information about community education available to all interested parties. Efforts along this line include workshops, conferences, presentations to school boards and other groups, seminars, and distribution of promotional materials and audio-visual aides.

Implementation was identified as the second center function and included consulting services and technical assistance to school districts in the process of implementing community education. Examples of activities which fall in this category are assistance with needs and resource assessment, locating funds, establishing and working with community councils, program planning and development, implementing agency coordination, determining goals and objectives, and evaluation procedures.

The third function was identified as training or those activities related to the development of community education leadership. Training efforts have included seminars, formal classes, workshops, fellowships, and other forms of pre-service and in-service activities.

It is important to note that the training function is highly dependent on the first two functions and on several other variables. The Foundation (1972) identified several of these variables:

1. Training needs are dependent upon the implementation of community schools nationally.
2. Training potential depends upon the willingness of universities and colleges to adjust their existing programs. Identification of willing institutions is imperative.
3. Training potential depends upon availability of competent leadership within the colleges and universities.
4. Training potential depends upon the availability of funds for the colleges to attract the needed leadership to their campuses. These funds are limited; therefore, maximum efficiency is important.
5. Much of the training called for in this plan is dependent upon the growth of Cooperating Centers. If this growth occurs, the training capacity can be realized. (pp. 41-42)

In addition to delineating the primary functions for the Centers, the five-year plan included a number of statistical projections for each of the fiscal years covered by the plan. These projections cover areas such as the numbers of: school districts with community education, community schools, cooperating centers established, masters and doctoral interns in community education, graduate students in formal community education classes, new community school directors, and states with supportive legislation.

OPERATION OF A CENTER FOR COMMUNITY EDUCATION

In examining the method of operation of the established centers, a variety of organizational patterns can be found. Seay (1974) reports organizational patterns such as direct responsibility to the dean of the college of education, responsibility to one department head within the college of education, responsibility to the dean of continuing education, and responsibility to the head of the department of recreation.

While each center is somewhat unique in its operation, a study by Procunier (1972) identified a number of conditions which are necessary for the successful operation of a center. These factors are: (a) proper leadership, (b) philosophical commitment, (c) an evident need, (d) financial support, (e) adjustable operating policies, (f) basic service capabilities, (g) intra-university communication, (h) university tradition, and (i) adequate office space.

If one looks at each of the centers, you will note that no two are identical in the methods used to carry out the three major functions. While each responds in a way which allows it to meet its own individual needs and to solve its own problems, there is some commonality in the goals established by each center. The goals developed by the staff of the Community School Development Center at Western Michigan University serve as an example of the ones used by many centers.

Goal I: Provide consultant services and assistance for school districts

Goal II: Provide preservice educational opportunities for community educators, lay personnel and students

Goal III: Provide in-service educational opportunities for community educators, lay personnel and students

Goal IV: Promote evaluation and research in community education

Goal V: Disseminate community education information

Goal VI: Promote the community education concept at the university level

Goal VII: Assist in the expansion of the community education concept at the state and national levels

DEVELOPMENT OF COOPERATING CENTERS

With a few exceptions, each of the regional centers has multi-state responsibility for the development of community education. An important aspect of this development is establishing cooperating centers for community education to serve a single state or in more populous areas, a part of a state. These cooperating centers are located not only in colleges and universities, but also in state departments of education and in one instance, a county department of education.

Development of this cooperating center network to work hand-in-hand with the regional centers seems to be a viable means to achieve the needed national dissemination, training, and consulting services. As the Foundation (1972) indicated in its long-range plan:

A major strength of cooperating centers seems to be that they can provide local assistance for public school systems. Because of their physical location, they can provide more immediate services and are in a better position to follow-up on initial contacts. By serving a smaller area, they are better able to understand state and local resources and conditions which contribute to the development of community education. Their location should contribute to a lower cost for the services they provide. Because of the time involved in travel, they are able to service more districts more economically within their smaller region. Since they serve fewer states, they are in an advantageous position of establishing meaningful relationships with state departments of education. (Appendix C)

In establishing a plan for a cooperating center, the Foundation (1972) has delineated the following minimal expectations:

1. A first year minimum of two-to-one financial match from sources other than Mott funds. This first year minimum should be surpassed each consecutive year.
2. Initially, there must be evidence of intention by the cooperating institution to carry on the community education center beyond the terminal date of seed money funds. At the midway point of the seed money period, there must be submitted to the sponsoring institution a resolution passed by the Board of Controls of the institution signifying acceptance of the Center as an integral part of the University operation and a commitment for support of the Center beyond terminal date of the Mott Foundation seed monies.
3. The cooperating institution shall be expected to present to the sponsoring center goals and objectives that will clearly identify the function of that cooperating center.
4. There must be evidence of public school need and acceptance of the community school concept in the area to be served by the cooperating center.
5. The cooperating center shall demonstrate a willingness and verbal commitment to develop strong working relationships with appropriate educational agencies to work toward community education becoming an integrated part of the state educational needs.[*]
6. The cooperating center must be committed to the establishment of undergraduate and graduate programs of instruction in community education.
7. The cooperating center must meet the training needs of community education in the area they serve.
8. There must be available within the university (cooperating center) physical and financial resources for the center.
9. The cooperating center personnel must have an assignment in one of the divisions of education, preferrably educational administration.
10. The cooperating center personnel must be fully within the tenure and promotional streams of the institutions with salary and other privileges commensurate with other staff members.
11. The cooperating center director should have a doctoral degree. He must have either spent a year in the National Center for Commu-

nity Education or a minimum of one semester full-time with a recognized Center for Community Education.
12. Prior to funding, the sponsoring institution shall incorporate the
above guidelines in a contractural-type agreement with the
cooperating institution. This contract shall be filed with the sponsoring institution and be available for review. (Appendix B)

It is expected that within a three to five year period those cooperating
centers which receive initial financial help from the Foundation will be able
to support their operation with funds from other sources.

THE FUTURE OF THE CENTER NETWORK

There are a number of factors which need to be considered when one
begins to examine the future of the center network. With the current five-
year plan terminating in 1978, many questions relative to the format for
continued financial support and philosophical commitment on the part of the
Foundation remain unanswered.

A development of 1976 which will most certainly influence the future is
the management/philosophy statement issued by the Foundation. In explaining the rationale for this statement, William S. White (1976), Foundation President states:

> The program purpose presented here restates past policies and princi-
> ples and in so doing builds upon the Foundation's past strengths. At the
> same time, the philosophy is designed to be flexible in order to meet
> unforeseen future needs. (p. 3)

The management/philosophy statement titled *Foundation for Living* is
divided into five sections which become the framework under which the
Foundation will function. The five sections are: (a) Governance, (b) Program Philosophy, (c) Program Policies, (d) Principles of General Management, and (e) Financial Guidelines. While each of the five sections has
relevance to the future of the center network, those dealing with Program
Philosophy and Program Policies seem to be most important.

Within the Program Philosophy, the following statement of purpose is
an important consideration:

> The purpose of the Mott Foundation is to identify and demonstrate
> principles which in application strengthen and enrich the quality of liv-
> ing of individuals and their community. Learning how men most effec-
> tively live together, or making community a practical reality, is one of
> the fundamental needs of mankind. (p. 5)

Based on this statement of purpose, four major principles and related mission statements were developed. Future grant making will be organized and interrelated on the basis of these principles which are: (a) opportunity for the individual, (b) partnership with the community, (c) effective functioning of community systems, and (d) leadership as the mobilizer. The mission statements under each of these principles are intended to give further direction to the Foundation's overall program philosophy.

The section dealing with Program Policies also has some implications for future Foundation involvement in community education. This section spells out the Foundation's position in areas such as where grants would normally go, grantee capability and priorities. These policies, together with the Program Philosophy outlined above, have direct linkages to future proposals and grants funded by the Foundation. These two sections, along with the other three, must be given due consideration when one looks at the future of the center network.

As this future unfolds, a number of questions remain unanswered. Will the Foundation continue its financial commitment to the regional center network? If yes, what will be the extent of this commitment? If no, can the regional center network survive? As cooperating centers no longer receive financial assistance from the Foundation, will they be able to secure adequate funding from other sources? As regional and cooperating centers are no longer tied to one another financially, what working relationships will develop? Is the national goal for community education as stated earlier still relevant? Should each region and/or each center develop its own goals and objectives based on the individual problems and uniqueness of the area served? Will another five-year plan be developed? If yes, what format should it take? If no, should some other form of long range plan be developed? Will the positions already created, especially in State Education Agencies, and the higher education training programs funded through existing federal dollars, be maintained when the legislation runs out? If no, what affect will this have on the national development of community education? Is there a need to more clearly define roles in states where both the State Education Agency and a center are attempting to carry out the functions of dissemination, technical assistance, and training? If yes, how can or should this be accomplished?

The challenge which lies ahead is one of seeking and finding answers to these questions and the multitude of others which surely influence the future direction of community education in the nation. What must be noted and stressed here is that one of the primary reasons for the national success of community education has been the emphasis and support given this concept by the Mott Foundation. The present as well as the coming years will see the fruits of these efforts across the country.

REFERENCES

C. S. Mott Foundation. *Foundation for living*. Flint, Mich.: C. S. Mott Foundation, 1976.

C. S. Mott Foundation. *Long range planning in community education*. Flint, Mich.: C. S. Mott Foundation, 1972.

Martin, G., & Seay, M. University involvement in community education. In M. Seay (Ed.), *Community education: A developing concept*. Midland, Mich.: Pendell Publishing Co., 1974.

Olsen, E. G., & Clark, P. A. *Life-centering education*. Midland, Mich.: Pendell Publishing Co., 1977.

Procunier, D. M. An analysis of factors necessary for effective innovation in regional community education dissemination centers (Doctoral dissertation, Michigan State University, 1972). *Dissertation Abstracts International,* 1972, *33*, 2044A-2045A. (University Microfilms No. 72-30,032)

"Indications are strong that success of state community education efforts is dependent on the effective functioning of the state education agency." — *Smith*

Chapter 22

Roles of the State Education Agency and the Federal Government in Community Education

by

Eric C. Smith

ROLES OF THE STATE EDUCATION AGENCY AND THE FEDERAL GOVERNMENT IN COMMUNITY EDUCATION

In the rather recent and widespread development of the community education concept across the United States, state education agencies are relative newcomers. Prior to 1975, only a handful of state departments of education had a staff specialist in community education. Initiation and development of local district programs within each state was coordinated through the Mott Foundation network of higher education regional and cooperating centers. The few state departments (early 1970's) with full-time state coordinators, (Minnesota, Utah) were also the states which initiated a state-funded assistance program to local school districts. Not until the mid-1970's did other states add full-time community education specialists to their staffs.

There are now over forty states each of which has a person hired on a full or part-time basis with the role as state coordinator or state liaison person. The primary factor which led to this rapid national growth was the federally funded Community Schools Act. This act designated one-third of the 3.5 million dollars for development of community education at the state education agency level. Consequently, many states have applied for and received funds for hiring personnel and for coordination of activities. While position descriptions and organizational structures vary, in many states the community education service is housed in the adult education section of the state department of education.

The role of state coordinator for community education is new enough that little has been written which defines the job role. In states which have developed a funded legislative package, one primary coordinator role is, quite naturally, one of developing guidelines and monitoring the use of state monies. The additional role responsibilities of a state education agency are: (a) to maximize its role in the development of community education; and (b) to establish a working relationship with the training centers housed in institutions of higher education and other related state agencies. The following are typical areas of role responsibilities:

1. develop a state plan for community education;
2. coordinate state level community education activities with related state agencies and institutions of higher education;
3. establish and maintain a state advisory council for community education;
4. provide technical assistance to local districts;

251

5. provide resource materials and promote statewide the concept of community education; and
6. evaluate and provide statistical summaries on the status of community education activities.

STATE PLAN

In a series of five federally-funded workshops held in 1976-77 hosted by the Texas A&M University Center for Community Education, state coordinators from throughout the United States met to discuss and gain an in-depth awareness of their job role. In addition to the many presentations, there was considerable discussion concerning the development of state plans. In most instances a state plan is developed from input solicited from diverse human service agencies, often through an established state advisory council.

State plans take various forms and the essence of such plans or the purposes for such plans vary. In general, a state plan is a document which attempts to define the structure and direction of community education in a given state. In addition, a state plan is a document suitable for promotion with state and legislative officials, for presentation to groups and agencies throughout the state, and for use as a guide to local districts interested in concept development. During discussions as the January 1977 workshop in Denver (State Education Agency Denver Seminar, 1977), the following were considered as primary elements in a state plan for community education:

1. rationale and definition of community education;
2. major long and short term goals for statewide development;
3. state advisory council role, membership and operation;
4. resources available to local districts;
5. technical advice on getting started with a local planning effort; and
6. role definition of key state agencies, including both the state department center and higher education training centers.

State plans can and do include other elements, depending on the state, its needs, and its level of development. Some of these more common elements might be: (a) state legislation (when it exists); (b) cooperative interagency agreements; (c) application procedures for state and/or federal funds; (d) facilities usage; and (e) any amount of specific, technical information on various program components.

STATE AGENCY COORDINATION

There are a multitude of human service agencies in any state which bear a relationship to the community education concept. The state education agency is the one agency which is in the best position to relate to the many agencies in fields such as aging, health, mental health, extension, professional associations, parks and recreation, adult education and many more. The form this contact takes will vary from an informational one to a more indepth arrangement of joint agreements and cooperative projects development. Part of the thrust toward cooperation would be to include key agency representation on the state advisory council.

Perhaps the most crucial relationship with any agency is the one between the state education agency and the one or more training centers in institutions of higher education. Each of these centers has a primary role responsibility in community education, yet several roles can and do overlap. Some primary roles might be:

State Education Agency

Coordination with state level agencies
State plan development
State Advisory Council
State legislation

Training Center

Graduate training program
In-service and pre-service workshops

Roles in which both agencies have a shared role are:

1. resource and dissemination services;
2. technical assistance to districts; and
3. presentations to various associations and conferences

In Wisconsin, both the state coordinator and the state training center director have developed a mutual set of cooperative goals and objectives (Cooperative Goal Agreement, 1977). This agreement not only identifies goals primary to each agency but also lists these goals, objectives and activities which are cooperative in nature. As a complement to this working arrangement, the two Wisconsin leaders have developed a common set of training materials, a common set of terminologies, and a cooperative arrangement regarding the mechanics for a statewide resource and dissemination service.

STATE ADVISORY COUNCIL

Most of the state agencies committed to hiring community education personnel have also established or are planning to establish state community education advisory councils. Typically the representation of these councils is a cross-section of agencies, professional associations, and lay representation. Most councils have between 15 and 21 members, serving one to two years each (Hayden, 1977).

The primary purpose of a state advisory council is to provide input and direction to the state community education section and state leadership. As a cross-representational body the advisory council is in a unique position. State training center directors, state department coordinator, and professional community educators, are all in a position to utilize the council as a sounding board and as a resource.

TECHNICAL ASSISTANCE

Technical assistance through a state education agency includes all those services to various communities and/or schools which lead to development of local community education programs. Initially the assistance might be in the form of in-service sessions for school and community groups. As programs develop and mature the assistance may take the form of in-service to local leadership on various program components, program evaluation, and providing information on new trends within and outside the state.

Technical assistance is a role which makes heavy demands on a state agency in terms of time and resources. As the numbers of community education districts grow, so should the resources which can provide technical assistance. Previously trained community educators, related state agencies, and regional cooperative units are all necessary elements in an expanding service capacity. A particularly useful resource is a strong professional association for community educators. In many instances this group, through regional and statewide conferences, is able to provide a valuable service in upgrading professional leadership skills.

RESOURCE AND DISSEMINATION CAPACITY

A wide range of materials, including films, books, pamphlets, and names of resource leaders, should be available on a free loan-out basis to interested persons. Quite often a more extensive resource capacity can be achieved through the cooperative arrangement of one or two central agencies. In Wisconsin a cooperative agreement by the State education agency and the State training center to establish a single statewide resource center was initiated.

A common role of many state education agencies is the regular distribution of a statewide newsletter. This type of newsletter can offer much in the way of keeping informational lines open and providing a focus for various community education developments throughout the state. A statewide newsletter should provide a coordinating function for various agency activities An appropriate part of this effort should be a calendar of events which highlights all community education and related activities.

STATISTICAL INFORMATION

State education agencies are in a position to act as a research and data collection agency for statewide community education activities. The state agency should collect and provide this statistical information as a means to justify and promote community education. Care must be taken in utilizing statistics. Models need to be developed which indicate the full range of the community education potential — process as well as program. Most efforts, to this point, have been largely unsuccessful in identifying and relating the importance of process elements, such as community coordinating functions and citizen involvement.

THE FEDERAL ROLE IN COMMUNITY EDUCATION

Though the role of the federal government was somewhat addressed in earlier sections of this chapter, it seems appropriate here to discuss this topic in greater depth. In 1974 the Federal Community Education Program was signed into law as part of amendments to the Elementary and Secondary Education Act. This legislation provided for a three-year funding cycle that would provide grants to: (1) state and local educational agencies to plan, establish, expand, improve, and maintain community education programs, and to provide developmental and technical assistance in connection with the establishment, expansion, improvement, and maintenance of community education programs; and (2) institutions of higher education to develop and establish, or expand, programs which will train persons to plan and operate community education programs.

As noted earlier, it was this federal legislation that provided the impetus for many state departments to initiate technical assistance and service to school districts involved in community education delivery. While the number of local school districts and state departments of education that have developed community education has grown significantly as a result of this federal support, even more important is the legitimizing aspect of the federal support. No longer can community education be considered to be outside the purview of the school, to be an add-on program that has no relevance to the other functions of the school. With the extension of federal support to community education programs, the concept of community education has come of age.

Thus, it seems that the chief functions served by the federal government in community education are three-fold: (1) to create interest and commitment to the concept in local school districts, state departments of education, and institutions of higher education; (2) to support the development of community education program delivery; and (3) to legitimize the concept of community education within the American philosophy of education. It is well to keep these in mind when considering other aspects of the practice of community education.

CONCLUSION

As with many other community education positions, the role of a state coordinator is one of extensive field activity. State coordinators' responses to a national survey indicated their top activity in community education efforts centered around on-site visitations. Most of their other efforts were spent in publicity, conference attendance, and conducting workshops (Department of Health, Education, and Welfare, 1976).

The role of a state education agency as an instrumental part of the state leadership team is a vital one. This is true not only in terms of the unique functions which can be provided but also in terms of the broadened base of state level leadership. Indications are strong that success of state community education efforts is dependent on the effective functioning of the state education agency. Impact of this leadership is shown by the growth in the number of states which have provided legislation and funding for community education. In 1976 there were twice as many states providing some state funding for community education as there were in 1974 (Department of Health, Education, and Welfare, 1976). There are 33 state agencies which have or are seeking some type of community education legislation (Department of Health, Education, and Welfare, 1976). The growth of community education parallels the growth of state education agencies. It seems certain that state education agencies will increase in size and influence as community education continues to grow.

REFERENCES

Cooperative goal agreement. (A document established by the state center for community education and the state training center). Madison, Wisc.: Wisconsin Department of Public Instruction, 1977.

Hayden, T. I. *S.E.A. advisory council survey.* Columbus, Ohio: Ohio State Department of Education, 1977.

Health, Education, and Welfare, Department of. *Community education at the state educational agency level.* Washington, D.C.: The Department of Health, Education, and Welfare, 1976.

State education agency Denver seminar. (One of five seminars hosted by the Community Education Center at Texas A&M University). College Station, Texas: Center for Community Education, Texas A&M University, 1977.

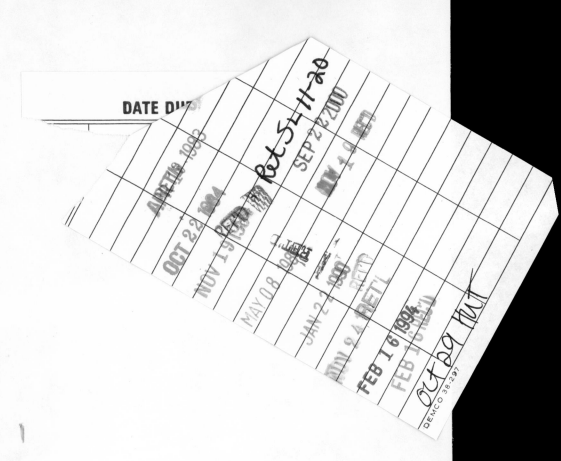